24-Hour
Sewing
Projects

by Linda Causee

Sterling Publishing Co., Inc.
New York

Produced by: The Creative Partners,™LLC

Book Design: Joyce Lerner

Photography: Carol Wilson Mansfield
James Jaeger

Technical Editing: Ann Harnden

Library of Congress Cataloging-in-Publication Data Available

10 9 8 7 6 5 4 3 2 1

Published by Sterling Publishing Co., Inc.
387 Park Avenue South, New York, NY 10016
© 2007 by The Creative PartnersTM LLC
Distributed in Canada by Sterling Publishing
c/o Canadian Manda Group, 165 Dufferin Street,
Toronto, Ontario, Canada M6K 3H6
Distributed in the United Kingdom by GMC Distribution Services,
Castle Place, 166 High Street, Lewes, East Sussex, England BN7 1XU
Distributed in Australia by Capricorn Link (Australia) Pty. Ltd.
P.O. Box 704, Windsor, NSW 2756, Australia

Sterling ISBN-13-978-1-4027-2316-2
ISBN-10: 1-4027-2316-4

For information about custom editions, special sales, premium and
corporate purchases, please contact Sterling Special Sales
Department at 800-805-5489 or specialsales@sterlingpub.com.

Enjoy your Sewing!

Just think of what you can make in just 24 hours or less—a lovely duvet cover, a quilt, a baby blanket, a tote bag—and every one of the projects in this great book.

To speed you along, I tell you how much time will be required to finish a project. Don't be dismayed, however, if it takes you longer. It's not a race. Whether you sew for just an hour a day, or for hours at a time, some of those precious hours will reward you with any of these projects.

For the Kitchen

Your kitchen doesn't have to be dull. In just a few minutes, you can create some wonderful additions to your kitchen, and also extend the excitement into your dining room.

Take a piece of novelty print fabric; add some borders, some batting, and you have created a beautiful wall hanging to add interest and beauty to your room.

Make a reversible apron to use while you're cooking. If cooking isn't your only hobby, make the reversible side mirror another hobby like gardening or winter sports.

Decorate your dining table with a patchwork table runner. Add a set of matching place mats, complete with a pocket to hold your matching napkins. Take the fabrics you used in your ensembles and create a pair of potholders that can be used to protect your hands from the heat or let them just hang as decorative accents to the room. How about a fabric bowl to hold your favorite fruits?

And finally, take some of the motifs from the wall hanging, affix them to purchased kitchen towels, and you've made something original and decorative, as well as useful.

fast, fun and fabulous projects

Perfect Picture Wall Hanging

"...a piece of novelty print fabric, add borders, some batting, and you have created a wall hanging."

time to make: about 3 hours

Approximate Size: 25" x 31"

Materials

3/4 yard novelty print fabric
1/4 yard yellow fabric (first border)
3/4 yard red fabric (second border and binding)
1 1/4 yards backing
craft size fusible batting
sewing thread and invisible monofilament thread

Cutting

1 rectangle, 18 1/2" x 24 1/2", novelty print
2 strips, 2" x 21 1/2", yellow (first border)
2 strips, 2" x 24 1/2", yellow (first border)
2 strips, 2 1/2" x 21 1/2", red (second border)
2 strips, 2 1/2" x 27 1/2", red (second border)
3 strips, 2 1/2" x 42", red (binding)
1 rectangle, 27" x 33", backing
1 rectangle, 27" x 33", batting
1 strip, 6" x 23", rod pocket

Instructions

Note: *Sew using a ¹/₄" seam allowance unless otherwise specified.*

1. Place 2" x 24¹/₂" yellow strip right sides together with right edge of novelty print rectangle; sew using a ¹/₄" seam allowance. Repeat on opposite side. (**Diagram 1**) Press seams toward yellow strip.

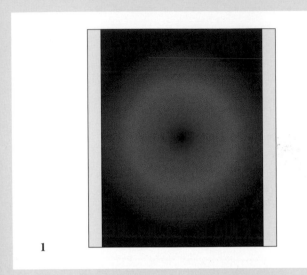

2. Place 2" x 21¹/₂" yellow strip right sides together with top edge of novelty print rectangle; sew using a ¹/₄" seam allowance. Repeat on bottom edge. (**Diagram 2**) Press seams toward yellow strip.

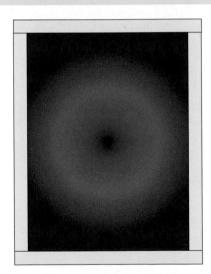

3. Repeat steps 1 and 2 using 2¹/₂" x 21¹/₂" and 2¹/₂" x 27¹/₂" red strips. (**Diagram 3**) Press seams toward red strips.

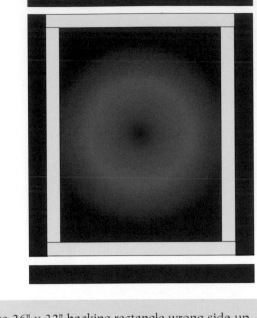

4. Place 26" x 32" backing rectangle wrong side up. Center fusible batting on backing and top right side up on batting. Following manufacturer's directions, fuse layers in place. **Note:** *The backing and batting are a little larger than the top.*

Quilt as desired using invisible monofilament thread.

5. Trim batting and batting even with top.

6. Refer to Attaching the Continuous Binding, page 141, to finish.

7. Refer to Adding a Rod Pocket, page 143, to attach a pocket to hang your wall hanging.

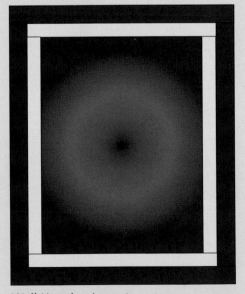

Wall Hanging Layout

Reversible Apron

"If cooking isn't your only hobby, make the reversible side mirror another hobby like gardening."

time to make: about 3 to 4 hours

Approximate Size: One size fits all

Materials
Note: *This apron is reversible.*
3/4 yard novelty print fabric A
1/4 yard coordinating fabric A
3/4 yard novelty print fabric B
1/4 yard coordinating fabric B
1/4 yard coordinating fabric C

Cutting
2 rectangles, 16" x 26", novelty print A
   (Apron Left and Right)
4 rectangles, 13" x 8 1/2", coordinating fabric A
   (Pocket)
2 rectangles, 16" x 26, novelty print B
   (Apron Left and Right reverse)
4 rectangles, 13" x 8 1/2", coordinating fabric B
   (Pocket reverse)
1 strip, 2 1/2" x 17", coordinating fabric C
   (Neck Strap)
1 strip, 2 1/2" x 20 1/2", coordinating fabric C
   (Neck Strap)
2 strips, 2 1/2" x 42", coordinating fabric 3 (Ties)

Instructions

Note: *Since the apron is reversible, work with one side at a time.*

1. Place novelty print A rectangles with right sides together on a flat surface. Measure and mark 13 1/2" up from the bottom right edge and 8" up from the bottom left edge. Mark 5 1/2" from left and right side of top edge. (**Diagram 1**)

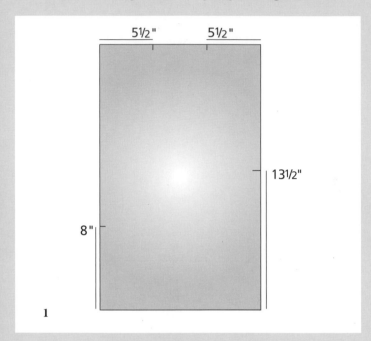

2. Draw a line from the marked left edge to the mark on the top left; draw another line from the marked right edge to the mark on the top right. (**Diagram 2**)

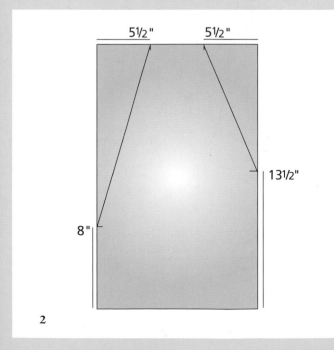

3. Cut along drawn lines for Apron Left and Apron Right. (**Diagram 3**)

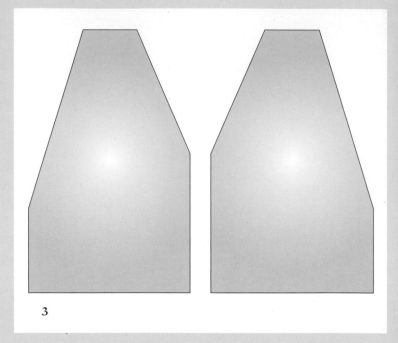

4. For pockets, place two coordinating fabric A rectangles right sides together; sew along all edges using a 1/2" seam allowance, leaving a 3" to 4" opening on one side for turning.

5. Turn pocket right side out through opening; hand stitch opening closed. Press pocket.

6. Repeat steps 4 and 5 for remaining pocket.

7. Center pockets on right side of Apron Left and Apron Right about 2 1/2" from the bottom edge. (**Diagram 4**) Pin in place.

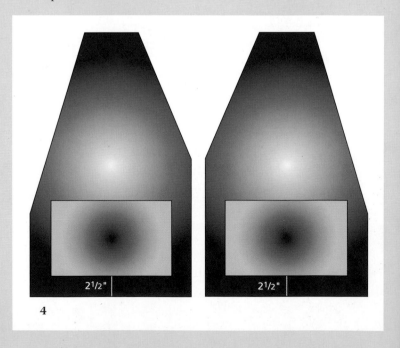

8. Sew pockets to Apron Left and Right along side and bottom edges. Sew down center of pockets to divide them into two sections. (**Diagram 5**)

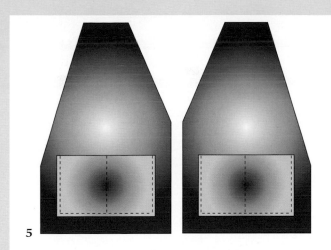

5

9. Repeat steps 1 to 8 for reverse side of apron using novelty print B and coordinating fabric B.

10. For Neck Straps and Ties, fold coordinating fabric C strips in half lengthwise with right sides together. Sew along entire length using a 1/4" seam allowance. (**Diagram 6**) Turn strips right side out and press.

11. Topstitch 1/4" from each long edge of each strip. (**Diagram 7**)

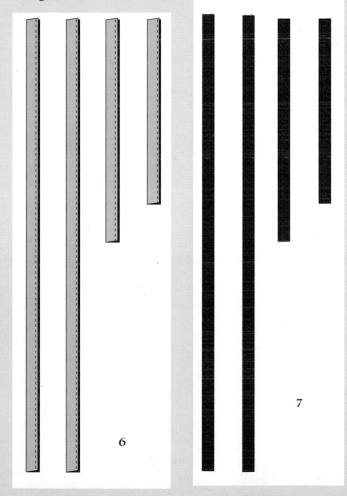

6

7

12. Measure 13 1/2" up from the bottom edge of both sides of Apron Left. (**Diagram 8**)

13. Pin a Tie on each side of Apron Left at the 13 1/2" mark. (**Diagram 9**)

14. Place Apron Left right sides together with Apron Left reverse. Sew along side and bottom edges using a 1/2" seam allowance and leaving top edge open. (**Diagram 10**) Be sure not to get loose ends of Ties caught in sewing. Turn Apron Left right side out and press.

15. Place Apron Right and Apron Right reversed right sides together; sew along side and bottom edges using a 1/2" seam allowance and leaving the top open. (**Diagram 11**) Turn Apron Right right side out and press.

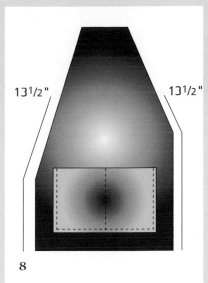

13 1/2"   13 1/2"

8

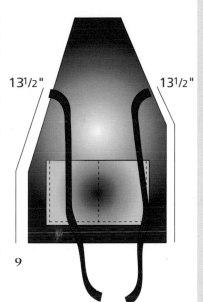

13 1/2"   13 1/2"

9

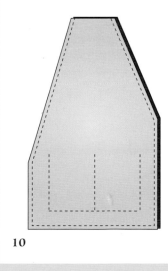

10

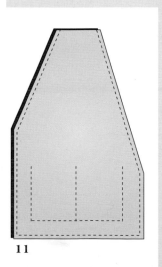

11

16. Fold in top edge of Apron Right and Left ½"; press.

17. Place Apron Left and Right next to each other on a flat surface. Tuck end of shorter Neck Strap ½" in top opening of Apron Left; tuck other end in top opening of Apron Right. (Diagram 12) Pin both ends in place.

18. Tuck end of remaining Neck Strap ½" in top opening of Apron Left; tuck other end in top opening of Apron Right. (Diagram 13) Pin both ends in place.

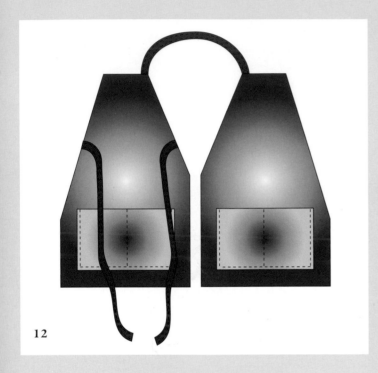

12

19. Sew across top edge of Apron Left and Right near folded edges catching the Neck Straps in the sewing. (Diagram 14)

20. Finish ends of Ties using a tight machine zigzag and matching thread.

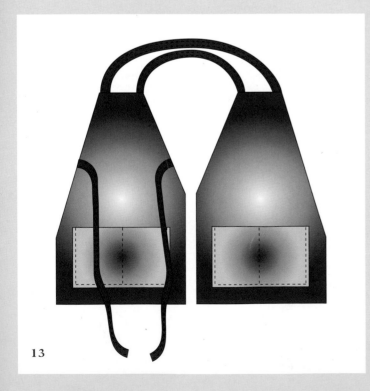

13

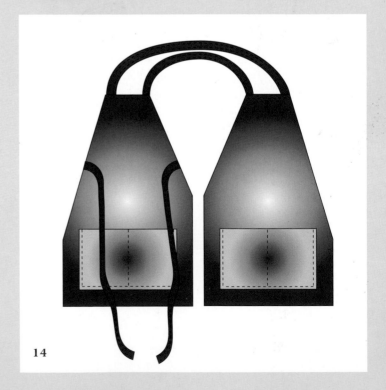

14

11

Patchwork Table Runner

"Decorate your dining table with a patchwork table runner."

time to make:
about 3-4 hours

Approximate Size: 12" x 36"

Materials

1/4 yard floral fabric
1/4 yard green fabric
1/4 yard yellow fabric
1/4 yard red fabric
1/2 yard black fabric (includes binding)
1/2 yard backing fabric
fusible batting
invisible microfilament thread

Cutting

2 strips, 2 1/2"-wide, floral
3 strips, 2 1/2"-wide, green
2 strips, 2 1/2"-wide, yellow
2 strips, 2 1/2"-wide, red
3 strips, 2 1/2"-wide, black
3 strips, 2 1/2"-wide, black (binding)
1 rectangle, 14" x 38", backing
1 rectangle, 14" x 38", fusible batting

Optional Method: *Making Nine-Patch blocks with strips is quicker than making them with individual squares. But, if you would like to make Nine-Patch blocks using squares rather than strips, cut the following:*

24 squares, 2 1/2" x 2 1/2", floral
24 squares, 2 1/2" x 2 1/2", green
12 squares, 2 1/2" x 2 1/2", yellow
24 squares, 2 1/2" x 2 1/2", red
24 squares, 2 1/2" x 2 1/2", black

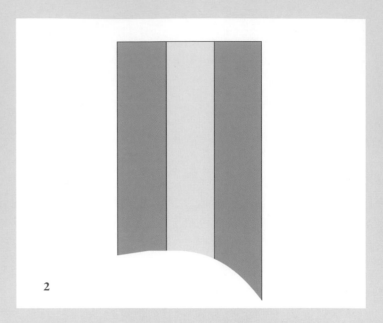

2

3. Cut strip sets at 2¹/2" intervals. You will need 12 cut strips from strip set 1 and six cut strips from strip set 2. (**Diagram 3**)

Instructions

Note: *Sew with a ¹/4" seam allowance.*

Nine-Patch Blocks

1. For strip set 1, place floral strip right sides together with a green strip; sew along length. Press seam toward floral strip. Sew a floral strip to opposite side of green strip. Press seam toward floral strip. (**Diagram 1**) Repeat for another strip set.

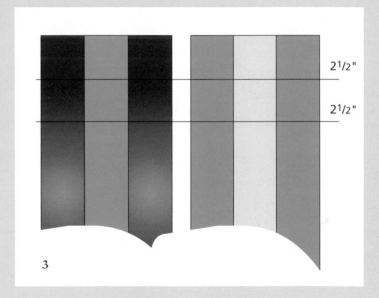

2¹/2"

2¹/2"

3

4. Place strip 1 and strip 2 right sides together; sew together. Sew another strip 1 to opposite edge of strip 2 to complete Nine-Patch block 1. (**Diagram 4**) Make six Nine-Patch 1.

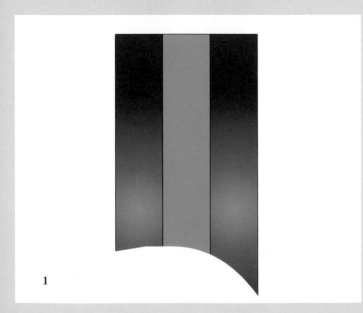

1

2. For strip set 2, place green strip right sides together with a yellow strip; sew along length. Press seam toward yellow strip. Sew a green strip to opposite side of yellow strip. Press seam toward yellow strip. (**Diagram 2**)

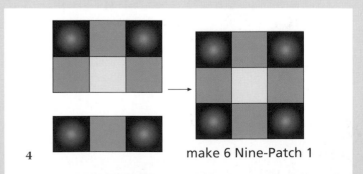

4

make 6 Nine-Patch 1

5. For strip set 3, place red strip right sides together with a black strip; sew along length. Press seam toward red strip. Sew a red strip to opposite side of black strip. Press seam toward red strip. (**Diagram 5**) Repeat for another strip set.

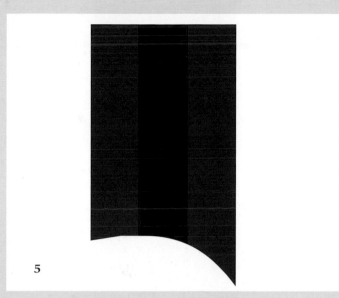

5

6. For strip set 4, place black strip right sides together with a yellow strip; sew along length. Press seam toward yellow strip. Sew a black strip to opposite side of yellow strip. Press seam toward yellow strip. (**Diagram 6**)

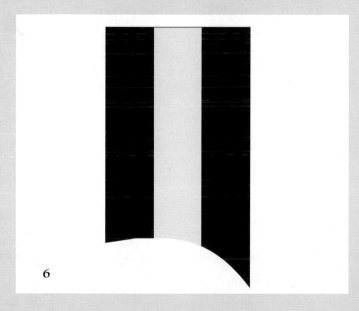

6

7. Cut strip sets at 2¹/2" intervals. You will need 12 cut strips from strip set 3 and six cut strips from strip set 4. (**Diagram 7**)

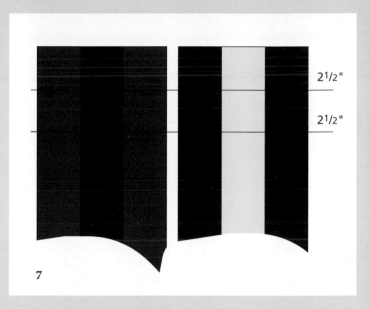

2¹/2"

2¹/2"

7

8. Place strip 3 and strip 4 right sides together; sew together. Sew another strip 3 to opposite edge of strip 4 to complete Nine-Patch block 2. (**Diagram 8**) Make six Nine-Patch 2.

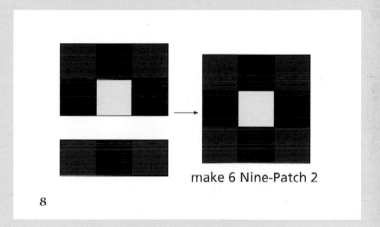

make 6 Nine-Patch 2

8

Optional Method:
Make Nine-Patch blocks with individual squares. Sew squares together in rows, then sew rows together. **(Diagram 9)**

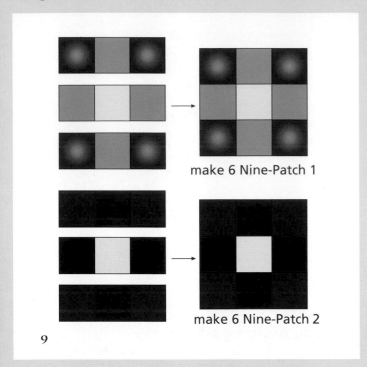

make 6 Nine-Patch 1

make 6 Nine-Patch 2

9

Finishing the Table Runner

1. Place a Nine-Patch 1 and Nine-Patch 2 block right sides together and sew. Press seam toward Nine-Patch 1. **(Diagram 10)** Repeat for five more pairs of blocks.

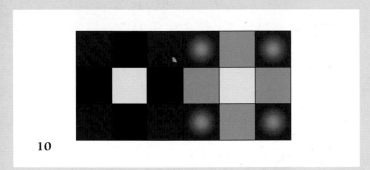

10

2. Sew pairs of Nine-Patch blocks together with adjacent pairs in opposite directions. **(Diagram 11)** Press seams to one side.

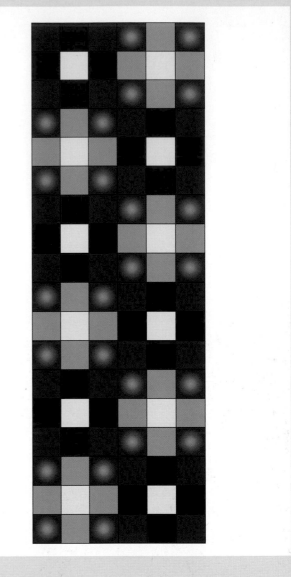

11

3. Place backing rectangle wrong side up. Center fusible batting rectangle on top and Table Runner top right side up on batting. Following manufacturer's directions, fuse layers together.

4. Using invisible monofilament thered, quilt in the seams between blocks to hold layers together. Trim batting and backing even with top.

5. Refer to Attaching the Continuous Binding, page 141, to finish Table Runner.

Matching Place Mat and Napkin

"...a set of...place mats, complete with a pocket to hold your matching napkins."

time to make: about 1 hour

Approximate Sizes:
  12" x 18" (Place Mat)
  17" x 17" (Napkin)

Materials
Note: *Materials for four Place Mats and four Napkins are in parentheses.*
  1/2 (1 1/4) yard floral fabric
  1/8 (5/8) yard green fabric
  1/4 (3/4) yard yellow fabric
  5/8 (2) yard black fabric
     (includes binding and backing)
  1 (4) rectangle, 14" x 20", fusible batting

Cutting
One Place Mat and Napkin
  4 squares, 2 1/2" x 2 1/2", floral
  16 squares, 2 1/2" x 2 1/2", yellow

16

8 squares, 2¹/₂" x 2¹/₂", black
1 rectangle, 6¹/₂" x 12¹/₂" yellow
8 squares, 2¹/₂" x 2¹/₂", green
1 rectangle, 6¹/₂" x 12¹/₂", green (pocket)
1 rectangle, 14" x 20", backing
2 strips, 2¹/₂"-wide, black (binding)
1 square, 18" x 18", floral (napkin)

Four Place Mats and Napkins
2 strips, 2¹/₂"-wide, floral
4 strips, 2¹/₂"-wide, yellow
3 strips, 2¹/₂"-wide, black
3 strips, 2¹/₂"-wide, green
4 rectangles, 6¹/₂" x 12¹/₂", yellow
4 rectangles, 6¹/₂" x 12¹/₂", green
4 rectangles, 14" x 20", backing
8 strips, 2¹/₂"-wide, black (binding)
4 squares, 18" x 18", floral (napkin)

Instructions

Note: *Sew using a ¹/₄" seam allowance unless otherwise specified.*

1. For a single Place Mat, make two each of two different Nine-Patch blocks. Sew a yellow square to opposite sides of a black square; repeat. (**Diagram 1**)

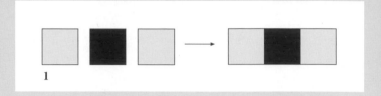

2. Sew a black square to opposite sides of a floral square. (**Diagram 2**)

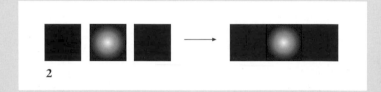

3. Sew the rows together to form a Nine-Patch block. (**Diagram 3**) Repeat for another block.

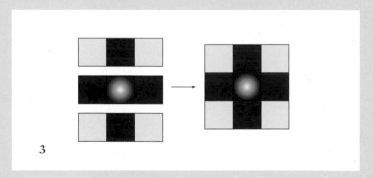

4. Repeat steps 1 to 3, except substitute green squares for the black squares. (**Diagram 4**)

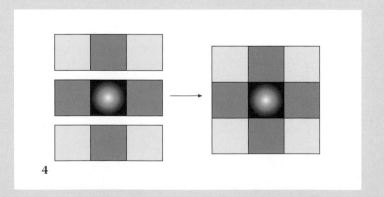

5. Sew a black Nine-Patch and green Nine-Patch together; repeat. (**Diagram 5**)

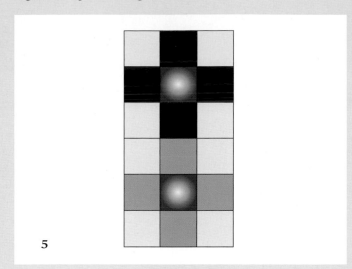

5

6. Fold the 6¹/2" x 12¹/2" green rectangle in half crosswise wrong sides together so that it measures 6¹/2" x 6¹/4". (**Diagram 6**)

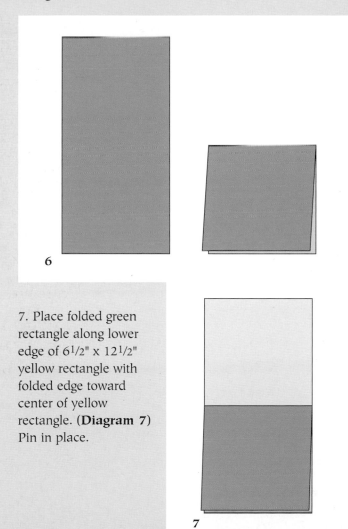

6

7. Place folded green rectangle along lower edge of 6¹/2" x 12¹/2" yellow rectangle with folded edge toward center of yellow rectangle. (**Diagram 7**) Pin in place.

7

8. Place a pair of Nine-Patch blocks right sides together with yellow rectangle. (Folded green rectangle will be in between.) Sew along one long edge. (**Diagram 8**) Press seam in one direction.

8

9. Sew remaining pair of Nine-Patch blocks to opposite side of yellow/green rectangle. (**Diagram 9**)

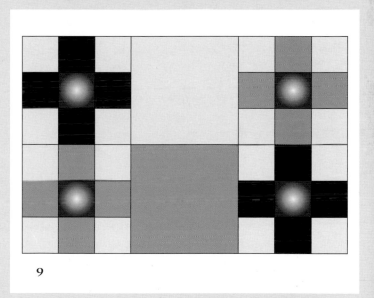

9

18

10. Place 14" x 20" backing rectangle with wrong side up. Place batting on backing, then center pieced top on batting. Referring to manufacturer's directions, fuse layers together.

11. Using invisible monofilament thread sew along seams of blocks to hold layers together. Be sure not to catch top of pocket in stitching.

12. Refer to Attaching the Continuous Binding, page 141, to finish Place Mat.

13. For Napkin, fold one edge of 18" floral square under 1/4", then another 1/4"; press. Stitch along fold. (**Diagram 10**)

14. Fold opposite edge of 18" floral square under 1/4", then another 1/4"; press. Stitch along fold.

15. Repeat along remaining two edges.

16. Fold Napkin and place in pocket of Place Mat.

10

Pretty Potholders

"...create a pair of potholders...to protect your hands from the heat or...as decorative accents to the room."

time to make:
about 1 1/2 hours

Approximate Size: 9" x 9"

Materials

1/4 yard floral fabric
1/8 yard green fabric
1/8 yard yellow fabric
1/4 yard black fabric
3/8 yard backing fabric
1/2 yard cotton batting
optional: 1" plastic drapery rings

Cutting

Potholder 1
  2 squares, 4" x 4", floral
      (cut squares in half diagonally)
  2 squares, 4" x 4", yellow
      (cut squares in half diagonally)
  4 squares, 3 1/2" x 3 1/2", floral
  1 squares, 3 1/2" x 3 1/2", green
  1 square, 9 1/2" x 9 1/2", backing
  2 squares, 9 1/2" x 9 1/2", batting
  1 strip, 2 1/2"-wide, black (binding)

Potholder 2
  2 squares, 4" x 4", green (cut squares in half
      diagonally)
  2 squares, 4" x 4", yellow (cut squares in half
      diagonally)
  4 squares, 3 1/2" x 3 1/2", floral
  1 squares, 3 1/2" x 3 1/2", green
  1 square, 9 1/2" x 9 1/2", backing
  2 squares, 9 1/2" x 9 1/2", batting
  1 strip, 2 1/2"-wide, black (binding)

Instructions

Note: *Sew using a ¼" seam allowance unless otherwise specified.*

Potholder 1

1. Place a floral triangle and a yellow triangle right sides together; sew along diagonal edge using a ¼" seam allowance. (**Diagram 1**) Press seam toward floral triangle.

1

2. Measure the resulting square and trim to 3½" x 3½" if necessary.

3. Repeat steps 1 and 2 for three more pairs of triangles.

4. Place pieced squares, floral squares and green square according to **Diagram 2**.

5. Sew the squares together in rows. Press seams in one direction for rows 1 and 3; press in the opposite direction for row 2. (**Diagram 3**)

6. Sew the rows together. (**Diagram 4**)

7. Place backing wrong side up, then both batting squares and pieced potholder on top. Pin layers together. Sew along seams between blocks to hold layers together.

8. Refer to Attaching the Continuous Binding, page 141, to finish potholder.

9. If you want to hang your potholder, sew a 1" plastic drapery ring at one corner.

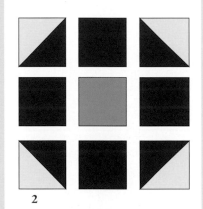

2

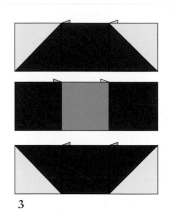

3

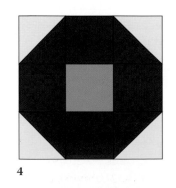

4

Potholder 2

1. Place a green triangle and a yellow triangle right sides together; sew along diagonal edge using a ¼" seam allowance. (**Diagram 5**) Press seam toward green triangle.

2. Measure the resulting square and trim to 3½" x 3½" if necessary.

3. Repeat steps 1 and 2 for three more pairs of triangles.

4. Place pieced squares, floral squares and green square according to **Diagram 6**.

5. Sew the squares together in rows. Press seams in one direction for rows 1 and 3; press in the opposite direction for row 2. (**Diagram 7**)

6. Sew the rows together. (**Diagram 8**)

7. Place backing wrong side up, then both batting squares and pieced potholder on top. Pin layers together. Sew along seams between blocks to hold layers together.

8. Refer to Attaching the Continuous Binding, page 141, to finish potholder.

9. If you want to hang your potholder, sew a 1" plastic drapery ring at one corner.

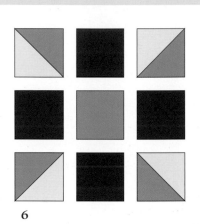

6

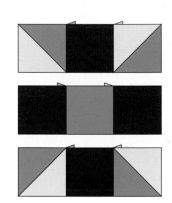

7

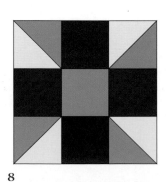

8

Decorative Towels

Some of the motifs from the wall hanging, affixed to purchsed kitchen towels, make something original and decorative.

12
9 3
6

time to make:
about 1/2 to 1 hour

Approximate Size: varies depending on size purchased

Materials
purchased kitchen towels
1/2 yard novelty fabric with individual motifs
1/4 yard coordinating or contrasting fabric
1/4 yard paper-backed fusible web

Cutting
1 strip, 3"-wide, coordinating or contrasting fabric

Instructions

1. Rough cut one or more motifs from the novelty print fabric. Following manufacturer's directions, fuse paper-backed fusible web to wrong side of novelty print motif. Cut out motif to desired size and shape. Fuse to front of towel at lower center. (**Diagram 1**) Finish raw edges by using a machine zigzag and coordinating or contrasting thread.

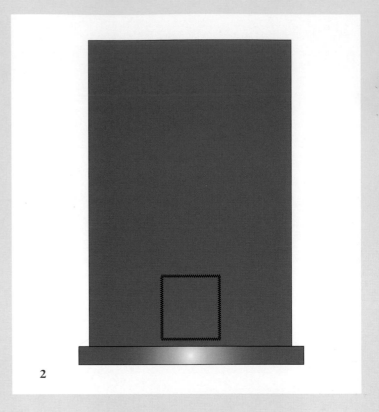

1

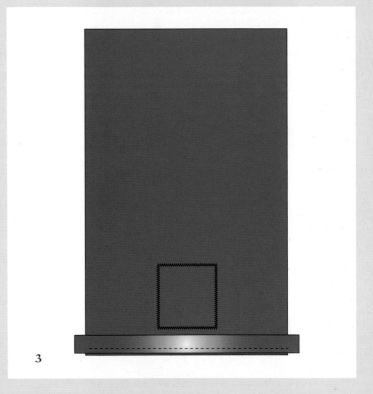

2

3

2. Measure the width of the towel and cut the 3"-wide strip that length plus 1". So if the towel width measures 10", cut the strip 11".

3. Cut off hem at one short edge of towel to reduce bulk. This will be referred to as the lower edge.

3. Fold the strip in half lengthwise with wrong sides together. Place along wrong side of lower edge with raw edges of strip even with edge of towel. Strip should overlap towel sides by 1/2" on each side. (**Diagram 2**)

4. Sew with a 1/2" seam allowance. (**Diagram 3**)

5. Fold strip toward front of towel; tuck ends in. Sew along fold of strip to finish towel.

Option

Finish entire edge of towel rather than one edge. First cut off hems at both short edges. Then, sew two 3"-wide strips together to make one long strip. Refer to Attaching the Continuous Binding, page 141, to finish towel.

Fruit Bowl

"How about a fabric bowl to hold your favorite fruits!"

time to make:
about 1 hour

Materials

fat quarter each outside fabric and inside fabric

12" square Fast-2-Fuse™ heavyweight fusible interfacing
   or Timtex™ heavyweight interfacing plus 5/8 yard
   paper-backed fusible web

matching thread

template plastic

permanent marker

removable fabric pen or pencil

Pattern

Fruit Bowl (page 25)

Instructions

1. Trace pattern onto template plastic using permanent marker. Turn template plastic and trace other half of pattern. Cut out template along drawn line. Trace and cut center circle template in same manner. (**Diagram 1**)

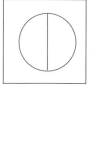

1

2. If using Timtex™, cut two squares larger than the outer dimension of the pattern from paper-backed fusible web. Fuse onto wrong side of dark and light print fat quarters.

3. Cut a square from Timtex™ the same measurements as the fused fabric from step 2. Remove paper backing and fuse fabric squares to each side of Timtex™ to form a three-layer unit.

4. If using Fast-2-Fuse™, cut two fabric squares from fabric and one from the Fast-2-Fuse™. Following manufacturer's directions, fuse fabric to both sides of Fast-2-Fuse™.

5. Place template on top of three-layer unit and trace using a removable fabric pen or pencil. (**Diagram 2**) Cut out along drawn line.

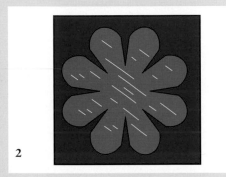

2

6. Place circle template in center of Fruit Bowl layers on inside fabric and trace. (**Diagram 3**)

3

7. Place unit under sewing machine needle. Set machine to a tight zigzag or satin stitch and sew slits. Begin sewing at inside point and sew toward outside edge butting up the edges as you sew. (**Diagram 4**) Repeat for all slits. This gives the bowl shape.

8. Form the base of the bowl by sewing satin stitches along drawn circle.

9. Satin stitch around entire outer edge of bowl to finish.

Fruit Bowl
1/2 Pattern

4

For the Baby in Your Life

The arrival of a new baby is the perfect occasion for you to get out your sewing machine and create something wonderful; do it quickly because babies grow fast.

The discovery of a novelty print that contained the letters of the alphabet was the impetus for creating the ABC quilt. If you can't find letters, any motifs will work. After making the ABC quilt, you won't be able to resist fusing the letters onto fleece fabric to create a quick receiving blanket.

To keep baby warm, take the fleece fabric and make baby a quick cap.

Every baby needs an entire wardrobe of receiving blankets, bibs and burp cloths. Make them quickly by sewing together squares of print novelty fabric and flannel, by fusing letters onto terry cloth and by sewing together squares of print and terry cloth.

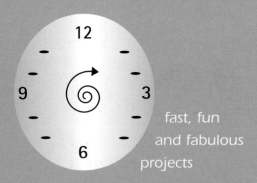

fast, fun and fabulous projects

Quickie Quilt

A novelty print that contains the letters of the alphabet inspired this ABC quilt for the new baby.

time to make:
about 7 hours

Approximate Size: 38" x 38"

Materials

1/2 yard novelty print fabric
   (photographed quilt uses an alphabet novelty print)
1/2 yard blue fabric
1/2 yard yellow fabric
1/4 yard green fabric
1/2 yard pink print fabric
crib-size batting

Cutting

Blocks

   36 squares, 3 1/2" x 3 1/2", novelty print
   36 strips, 1 1/2" x 3 1/2", yellow
   36 strips, 1 1/2" x 3 1/2", blue
   36 strips, 1 1/2" x 5 1/2", yellow
   36 strips, 1 1/2" x 5 1/2", blue

Finishing

   2 strips, 1 1/2" x 30 1/2", green (first border, sides)
   2 strips, 1 1/2" x 32 1/2", green
      (first border, top and bottom)
   2 strips, 3 1/2" x 32 1/2", pink print
      (second border, sides)
   2 strips, 3 1/2" x 38 1/2", pink print
      (second border, top and bottom)
   4 strips, 2 1/2"-wide by width of fabric, yellow (binding)

Instructions

Note: *Sew using 1/4" seam allowance throughout.*

1. Sew 1½" x 3½" blue strips to opposite sides of novelty print squares. (**Diagram 1**) Press seams toward blue strips.

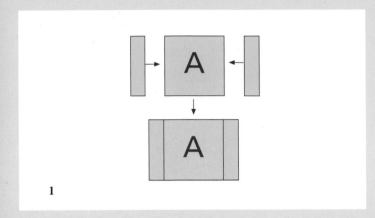

1

2. Sew 1½" x 5½" blue strips to remaining sides of squares. (**Diagram 2**) Press seams toward blue strips. Repeat for 17 more squares.

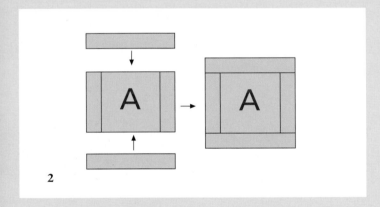

2

3. Sew 1½" x 3½" yellow strips to opposite sides of novelty print squares. (**Diagram 3**) Repeat for 17 more squares. Press seams toward yellow strips.

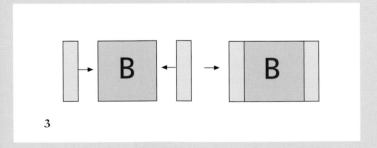

3

4. Sew 1½" x 5½" yellow strips to remaining sides of squares. (**Diagram 4**) Press seams toward yellow strips.

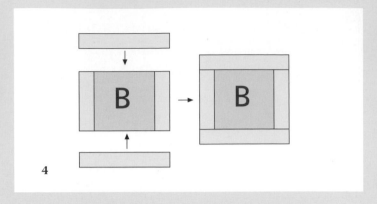

4

5. Place blocks in six rows of six blocks each, alternating blue and yellow framed blocks. (**Diagram 5**)

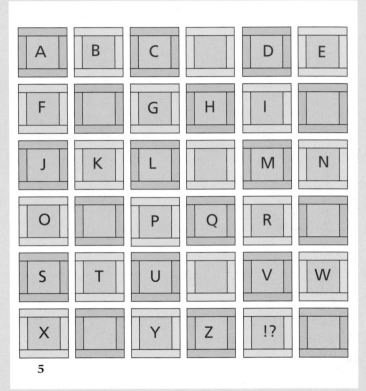

5

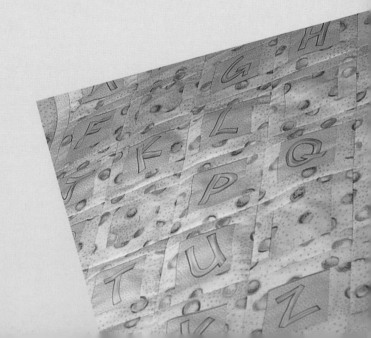

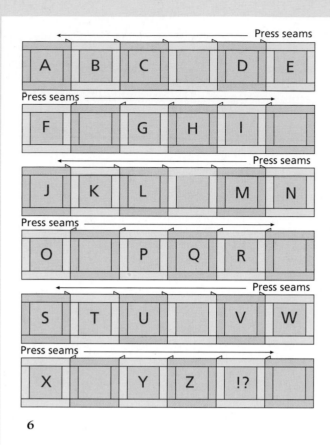

Press seams → A B C D E

Press seams → F G H I

Press seams → J K L M N

Press seams → O P Q R

Press seams → S T U V W

Press seams → X Y Z !?

6

6. Sew blocks in rows. Press seams for rows in opposite directions. (**Diagram 6**)

7. Sew rows together. Press quilt top.

8. Sew 1 1/2" x 30 1/2" green strips to opposite sides of quilt top. Sew 1 1/2" x 32 1/2" green strips to top and bottom of quilt top. Press seams toward border strips. (**Diagram 7**)

9. Sew 3 1/2" x 32 1/2" pink print strips to opposite sides of quilt top. Sew 3 1/2" x 38 1/2" pink print strips to top and bottom of quilt top. (**Diagram 8**)

10. Refer to Making a Quilt, pages 137 to 142 to finish your quilt.

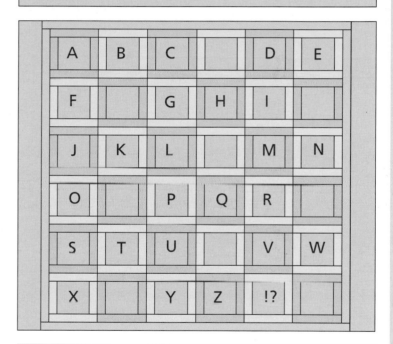

8

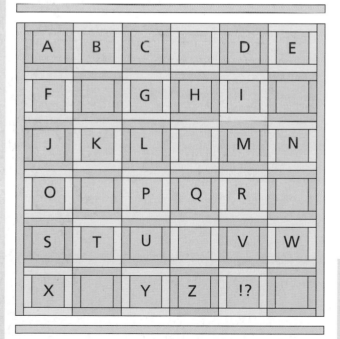

7

A	B	C		D	E
F		G	H	I	
J	K	L		M	N
O		P	Q	R	
S	T	U		V	W
X		Y	Z	!?	

Quickie Quilt Layout

Baby's Blanket and Bonnet

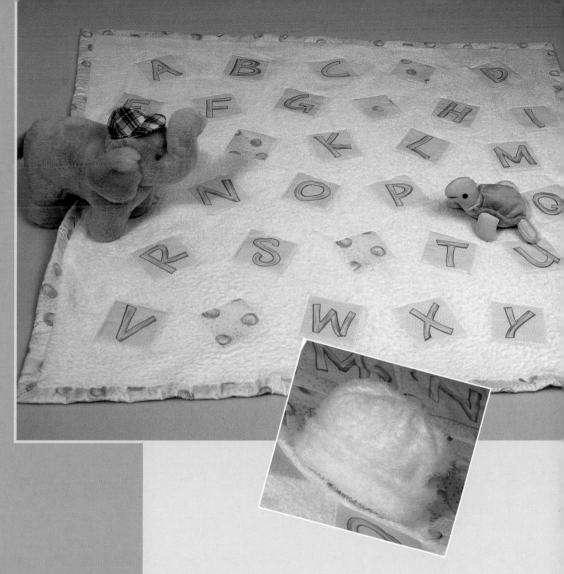

Fuse the letters like those in the Quickie Quilt onto fleece fabric and create a receiving blanket. Add a quick bonnet to complete the outfit.

time to make: about 3 1/2 hours

Approximate size: 36" x 36"

Materials
1 yard fleece
1/2 yard baby novelty print fabric
1/2 yard coordinating print fabric
1/2 yard lightweight paper-backed fusible web

Cutting
Blanket
one square, 36" x 36", fleece
*33 squares, 3" x 3", baby novelty print
four strips, 4"-wide, coordinating print
*Fuse novelty print to paper-backed fusible web according to manufacturer's directions before cutting squares.

Bonnet
1 rectangle, 10" x 18", fleece

Instructions
Blanket

1. Arrange fusible novelty print squares on 36" fleece square. Alternate rows of six and five squares. (**Diagram 1**)

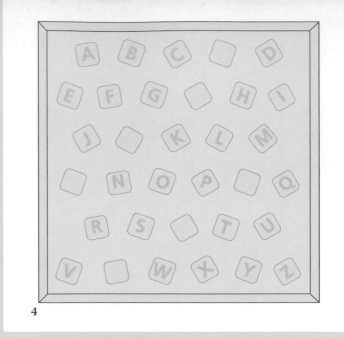

4

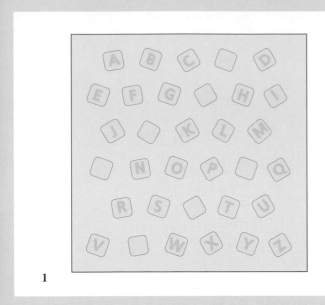

1

2. Fuse squares to fleece, then machine zigzag around squares using matching thread.

3. Sew 4"-wide strips together to make one long strip. Press seams open. (**Diagram 2**)

4. Fold strip in half lengthwise with wrong sides together. (**Diagram 3**)

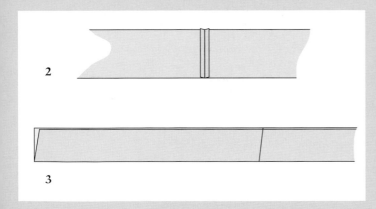

2

3

5. Refer to Attaching the Continuous Binding, page 141, to attach folded strip, except use a $1/2$" seam allowance and fold strip 1" toward front. (**Diagram 4**)

Bonnet

1. Fold fleece rectangle in half along short side. Sew along short edge using a $1/2$" seam allowance. (**Diagram 1**)

2. Sew two rows of long basting stitches $1/8$" and $1/4$" from one raw edge. (**Diagram 2**)

3. Pull thread ends of both basting rows to gather to about 2". (**Diagram 3**) Tie thread ends into a knot. Tie again to reinforce.

4. Fold opposite edge under 3". Sew along raw edge. (**Diagram 4**)

5. Turn hat right side out.

6. Hand stitch along gathered stitches at top of hat to close opening.

7. Fold lower edge up $1 1/2$" to finish.

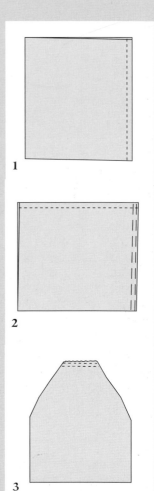

1

2

3

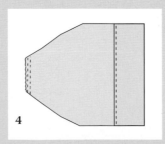

4

Baby's Three B's

All babies need the Three B's: blankets, bibs and burp cloths.

time to make:
about 2 hours

Approximate Blanket Size: 36" x 36"

Materials
1 yard yellow flannel fabric
1¼ baby novelty print fabric
2 fat quarters assorted baby novelty prints fabrics
¼ yard each, pink, blue, and yellow terry cloth
3 packages mutli-colored pastel large rickrack
*1-3 package double-fold bias binding
   (coordinating or contrasting colors)
*The same colored bias binding or a different color for each can be used for all bibs.

Patterns
Bib (page 38)
ABC Letters (page 38)

Cutting
Blanket
   1 square, 36" x 36", yellow flannel
   1 square, 36" x 36", baby novelty print
Bibs
   1 bib each, pink, blue, and yellow terry cloth
   2 bibs, baby novelty print
Burp Cloths
   1 rectangle each, 12" x 18", pink, blue, and yellow
     terry cloth
   1 rectangle each, 12" x 18", assorted novelty prints

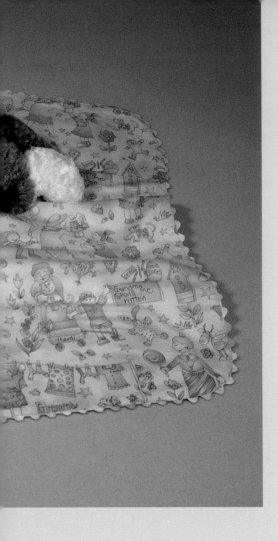

Instructions

Blanket

1. Sew rickrack along raw edge of right side of 36" novelty print square. At corners, curve rickrack and continue sewing. (**Diagram 1**)

2. Place novelty print square right sides together with 36" flannel square. Sew along previous sewing line leaving an opening for turning. (**Diagram 2**) Trim corners close to rickrack edge.

3. Turn blanket right side out through opening. Topstitch along edge of blanket near rickrack. (**Diagram 3**)

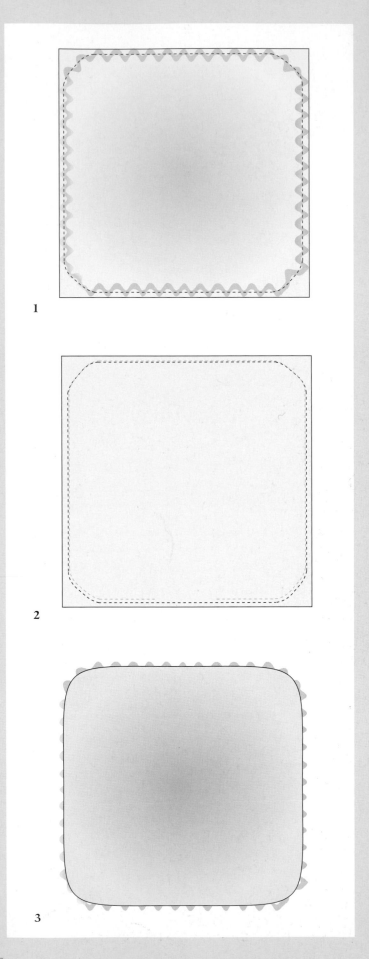

1

2

3

Bibs

Pink Bib:

1. Trace ABC letters onto paper side of fusible web. Fuse paper-backed fusible web to wrong side of baby novelty print. Cut out letters.

2. Fuse letters onto pink terry cloth bib.

3. Sew double-fold bias binding to lower edge of bib. **(Diagram 1)**

1

4. Cut a 24" length of bias binding and sew to top edge of bib to finish. **(Diagram 2)**

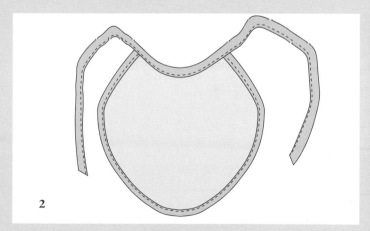

2

Blue Bib:

1. Place novelty print bib right sides together with terry cloth bib. Sew along lower edge of bib using a 1/4" seam allowance. **(Diagram 3)**

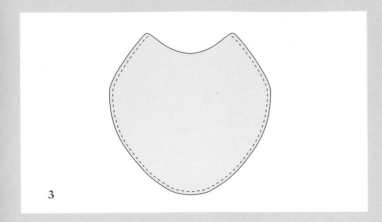

3

2. Turn bib right side out and topstitch about ¼" from sewn edge. **(Diagram 4)**

4

3. Cut a 24" length of bias binding and sew to top edge of bib. **(Diagram 5)**

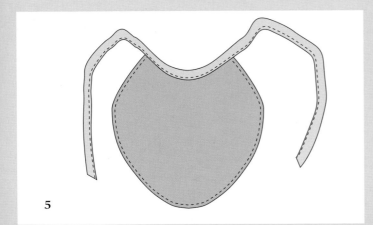

5

Yellow Bib

1. Sew rickrack along lower edge of novelty print bib.

2. Place novelty print bib right sides together with terry cloth bib. Sew along previous stitching. **(Diagram 6)** Turn bib right side out.

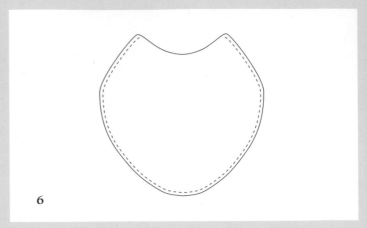

6

3. Cut a 24" length of bias binding and sew to top edge of bib. **(Diagram 7)**

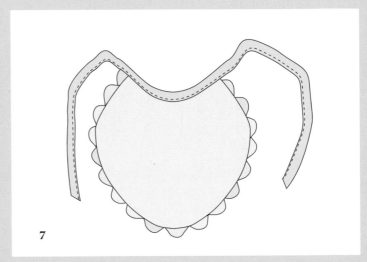

7

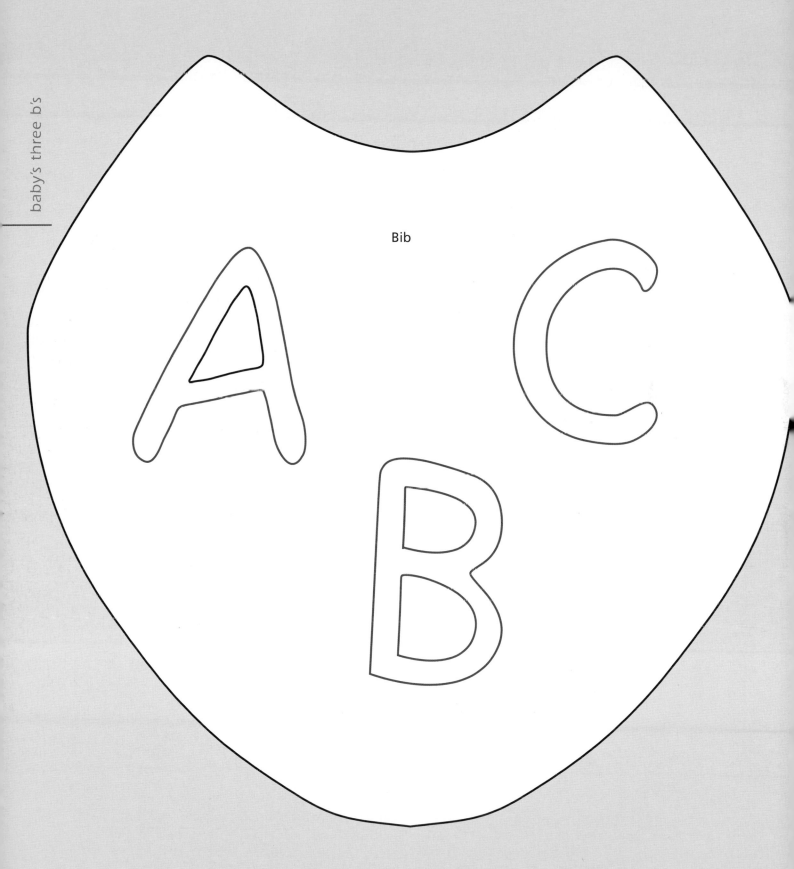

Bib

Burp Cloths

1. Place novelty print rectangle right sides together with terry cloth rectangle. Sew along all sides curving at corners and leaving an opening for turning. (**Diagram 1**)

2. Turn right side out and whipstitch opening closed.

3. Topstitch 1/4" from all edges. (**Diagram 2**)

Finishing Options:

1. Sew rickrack to novelty print rectangle before sewing to terry cloth rectangle.

2. Sew single-fold bias binding along all edges.

3. Use a decorative machine stitch along edges of rectangle.

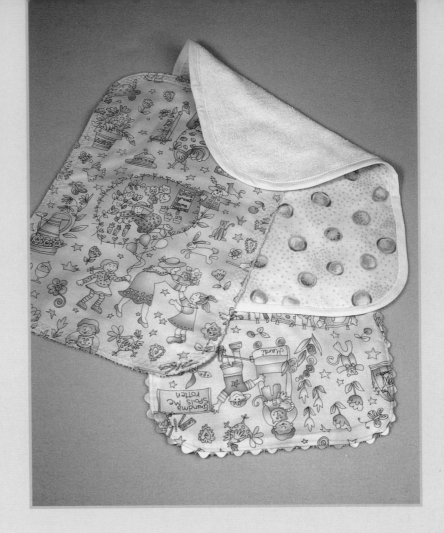

1

2

For the Bathroom

Think you can't make your bathroom a show place? Think again. With just some fabric and a little bit of time, you can turn an everyday bathroom into a decorator's dream.

Add some fabric trim onto your towels to create some truly unique items. Display your tissues in a matching tissue box.

And for those special soaps that you tend to hide in a cabinet, make a fabric "Show Off the Soap" dish that matches your towels and tissue box.

Beautiful!

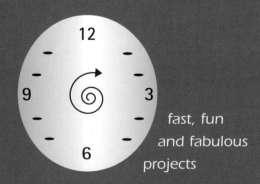

fast, fun and fabulous projects

Terrific Towels

"Add some fabric trim onto your towels to create some truly unique items."

time to make:
about 2 hours

The photographed bath and hand towel set shows two different finishing variations. You can make your set as shown or make both pieces with the same finishing.

Materials
purchased bath towel
purchased hand towel
3/4 yard border print fabric
1/4 yard pink print fabric (binding)
1/4 yard fabric with individual floral motifs
1/4 yard blue floral print fabric (ruffle)
3/4 yard paper-backed fusible web
invisible or matching thread

Instructions

Bath Towel

1. Choose a border strip that is about 3" to 4" wide, then cut a strip from the border print the width of the towel plus 1". For example, if the towel is 20" wide, cut the border strip 21" long. Iron paper-backed fusible web to wrong side of border print strip following manufacturer's directions.

2. Fuse border print to lower end of towel about 2 1/2" from bottom, folding short ends toward back of towel. (**Diagram 1**) Finish raw edges using a machine zigzag and matching or invisible thread.

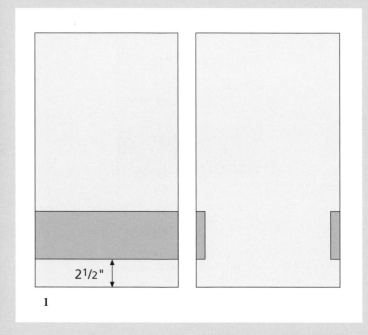

2 1/2"

1

3. For ruffle, cut a 5"-wide strip across the width of the blue floral print fabric. (Strip will be about 42" to 44" long.) Fold short edges of 5"-wide blue floral pint strip under 1/4", then another 1/4". Sew along first fold. (**Diagram 2**)

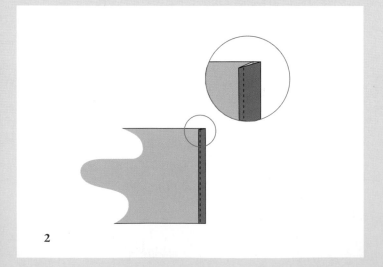

2

4. Fold ruffle strip in half lengthwise with wrong sides together. Using a long basting stitch, sew two rows of stitching 1/4" and 5/8" from raw edges. (**Diagram 3**)

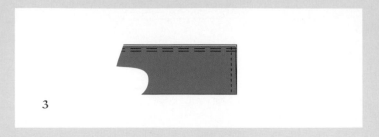

3

5. Pull threads to form ruffle to fit width of towel.

6. Pin ruffle to lower end on right side of the towel; raw edge of ruffle should be about 1" from lower edge of towel. (**Diagram 4**)

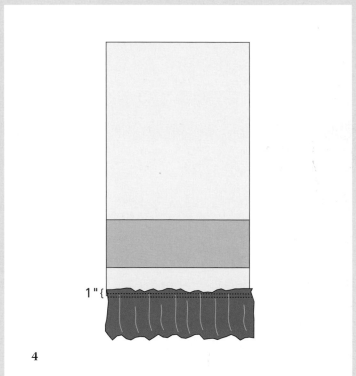

1"{

4

7. For binding, cut a 2¹/₂"-wide strip across width of pink print fabric. Then cut that strip the width of the towel plus 1". (For example, if the towel is 15" wide, cut the strip 16" long.) Fold pink print strip in half with wrong sides together. Place folded strip on top of ruffle with raw edges even and each end extending ¹/₂" past sides of towel. **(Diagram 5)**

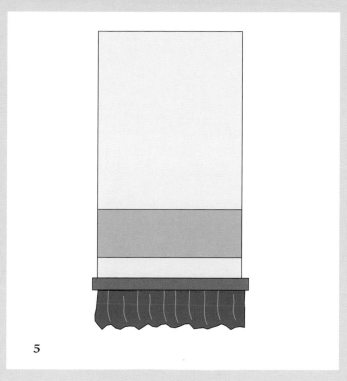

5

8. Sew all layers together ³/₈" to ¹/₂" from raw edges. **(Diagram 6)**

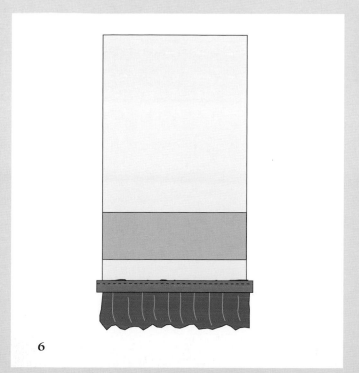

6

9. Fold pink print strip over the seam allowance and tuck ends under so they are even with side edges of towel. Sew along fold of pink print strip using a machine zigzag stitch and invisible or matching thread. **(Diagram 7)**

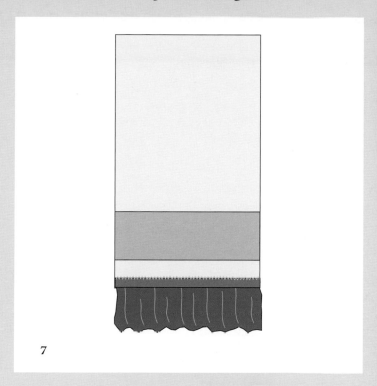

7

10. Make a matching hand towel by following steps 1 to 9 above except cut the blue floral ruffle strip 4" wide.

Hand Towel

1. Cut a strip from the border print fabric that is the width of the hand towel plus 1". Iron paper-backed fusible web to wrong side of border print strip following manufacturer's directions.

2. Fuse border print to lower end of towel about 2" from bottom, folding short ends toward back of towel. (**Diagram 1**) Zigzag along both raw edges.

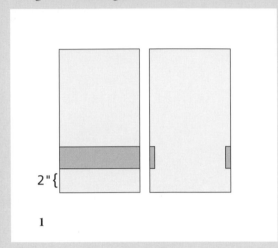

1

3. Fuse a piece of paper-backed fusible web to back of floral motif. Cut out motif, then fuse to towel centered on border strip. (**Diagram 2**) Zigzag along raw edges using invisible or matching thread.

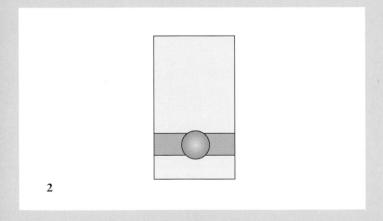

2

4. Cut a 2¹/₂"-wide strip from pink print fabric. Cut into two strips the width of the hand towel plus 1".

5. Fold one strip in half lengthwise with wrong sides together. (**Diagram 3**)

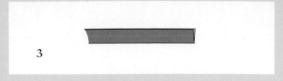

3

6. Place folded strip along short edge of wrong side of towel with raw edges even with edge of towel and short ends extending ¹/₂" past sides of towel. Sew using a ¹/₄" seam allowance. (**Diagram 4**)

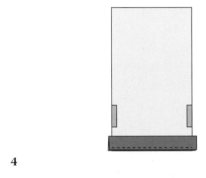

4

7. Fold pink print strip forward over edge of towel. Tuck short ends under and sew pink print strip to towel along folded edge using a zigzag stitch and matching or invisible thread. (**Diagram 5**)

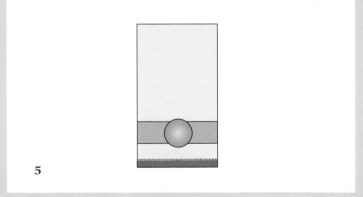

5

8. Repeat steps 5 to 7 for opposite short end of towel.

9. Repeat steps 1 to 8 for bath towel to match hand towel.

Dressed-Up Tissue Box

"With some fabric...you can turn an everyday bathroom into a decorator's dream."

time to make:
about 2¹/₂ hours

Materials
purchased boutique tissue box
fat quarter dark blue floral print fabric (sides)
7" square contrasting print fabric (top)
¹/₄ yard light print fabric (lining)
¹/₄ yard floral print fabric (ruffle)
*¹/₄ yard fusible batting
*Using fusible batting will make sewing easier, but you can also use a thin cotton of polyester batting. Instead of fusing the layers together you will need to pin or baste to hold them together for sewing.

Cutting
4 rectangles each, 5³/₄" x 6¹/₂", dark blue floral print, batting, light print (sides)
2 rectangles each, 3³/₈" x 5³/₄", contrasting print, batting, light print (top)
1 strip, 4¹/₂"-wide, dark blue floral print (ruffle)

Instructions

1. For top, place 3³/₈" x 5³/₄" light print rectangle wrong side up; place batting on top, then put contrasting print rectangle right side up on top of batting. Fuse layers together following manufacturer's directions.

2. Place the fused top rectangle layers sides together. Sew 1¹/₂" along long edge using ¹/₂" seam allowance; leave a 2³/₄" gap and sew for another 1¹/₂". **(Diagram 1)**

3. To finish top opening, trim batting and light print (lining) portion of the seam allowance to about ¹/₄". Fold contrasting print seam allowance to cover cut raw edges. Press seam open. Sew seam allowance to top near folded edges. **(Diagram 2)**

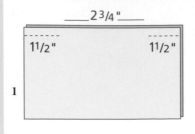

1

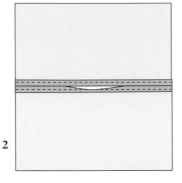

2

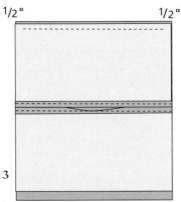

3

4. For sides, place 5³/₄" x 6¹/₂" light print rectangle wrong side up; place batting on top, then put dark blue floral rectangle right side up on top of batting. Fuse layers together following the manufacturer's directions.

5. Place a fused side rectangle right sides together with fused top; sew using a ¹/₂" seam allowance beginning and ending sewing ¹/₂" from each end. **(Diagram 3)**

6. Repeat step 5 for remaining three fused side rectangles on remaining three sides of top.

7. Sew sides together using a ¹/₂" seam allowance and beginning ¹/₂" from the top.

8. Trim seam allowances to about ¹/₄". Serge or zigzag raw edges of seam allowances.

9. For ruffle, fold strip in half crosswise with right sides together and sew short ends together to form a tube. **(Diagram 4)**

4

10. Fold tube in half lengthwise with wrong sides together. **(Diagram 5)**

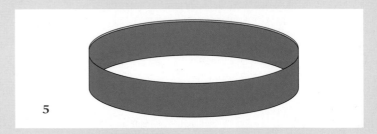

5

11. Using a basting stitch, sew ¹/₄" and ⁵/₈" from raw edges. **(Diagram 6)**

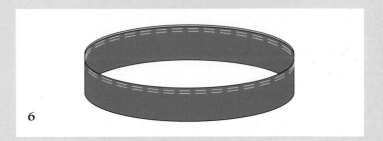

6

12. Pull thread ends to form a ruffle to fit the lower edge of tissue box cover.

13. Pin ruffle to lower edge of tissue box holder adjusting ruffle so the folds are evenly distributed along all four sides. Sew using a ¹/₂" seam allowance.

14. Trim seam allowance to about ¹/₄" and machine zigzag along raw edges.

15. Topstitch lower seam allowance above ruffle to tissue box cover. **(Diagram 7)**

7

Show Off the Soap Dish

Make a fabric soap dish for those special soaps that you tend to hide in a cabinet.

time to make: about 1 hour

Approximate Size: 6" x 9"

Materials

fat quarter each outside fabric and inside fabric
12" square Fast-2-Fuse™ heavyweight fusible interfacing or Timtex™ heavyweight interfacing plus 5/8 yard paper-backed fusible web
matching thread
template plastic
permanent marker
removable fabric pen or pencil

Pattern

Show Off the Soap Dish (page 49)

Instructions

1. Trace outer Soap Dish pattern and center oval pattern onto template plastic using permanent marker. Cut out templates along drawn line.

2. If using Timtex™, cut two rectangles larger than the outer dimension of the pattern from paper-backed fusible web. Fuse onto wrong side of dark and light print fat quarters.

3. Cut a rectangle from Timtex™ the same measurements as the fused fabric from step 2. Remove paper backing and fuse fabric rectangles to each side of Timtex™ to form a three-layer unit.

4. If using Fast-2-Fuse™, cut two fabric rectangles from fabric and one from the Fast-2-Fuse™. Following manufacturer's directions, fuse fabric to both sides of Fast-2-Fuse™.

5. Place outer template on top of three-layer unit and trace using a removable fabric pen or pencil. (**Diagram 1**) Cut out along drawn line.

1

6. Place oval template in center of soap dish layers on inside fabric and trace. (**Diagram 2**) Remove Template.

7. Place unit under sewing machine needle. Set machine to a tight zigzag or satin stitch and sew slits. Begin sewing at inside point and sew toward outside edge butting up the edges as you sew. (**Diagram 3**) Repeat for all slits. This will give the soap dish its shape.

2

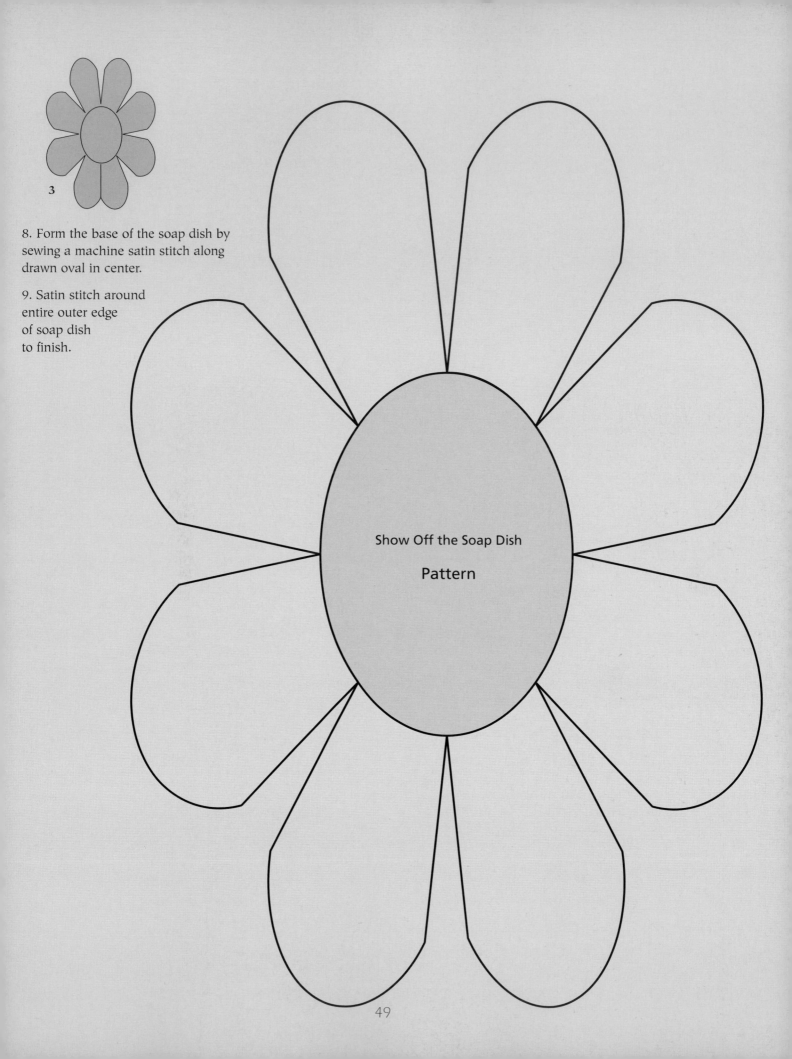

3

8. Form the base of the soap dish by sewing a machine satin stitch along drawn oval in center.

9. Satin stitch around entire outer edge of soap dish to finish.

Show Off the Soap Dish

Pattern

For the Bedroom

A beautiful duvet cover, lovely pillow shams and a group of pillows make the bedroom an ideal show place.

Join a series of rectangles cut from various matching fabrics including faux suede into a fabulous-looking top. Use a king-size flat sheet as the backing, and your elegant duvet cover is complete. Join another group of rectangles into matching pillow shams.

Five different shapes of pillows add the finishing touch. Make a simple Four Patch pillow into a conversation piece with a beaded trim. Simple fringe decorates one pillow and a round pillow is crowned with an easy-to-make rosebud. Wide ribbon decorates the Neck Roll pillow while fringe and a brooch or decorative button complete the Envelope pillow.

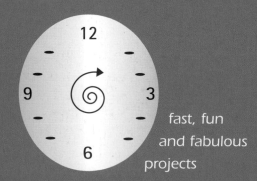

fast, fun
and fabulous
projects

Duvet Cover and Pillow Shams

Rectangles cut from matching fabrics including faux suede make a beautiful duvet cover that turns the bedroom into and ideal show place.

time to make: about 6 hours

Approximate Size: Duvet Cover 101 1/2" x 90"
Shams 31" x 25"

Materials
Duvet Cover and two Shams
   2 1/2 yards light blue fabric
   2 yards medium blue faux suede
   1 1/2 yards dark blue fabric
   1 yard blue floral fabric
   1 1/2 yards off-white fabric
   2 yards blue stripe fabric
   king-size flat sheet (duvet cover backing)
   12 velcro squares (1" square)
   1 3/4 yards blue solid (sham backing)

Cutting
Duvet Cover
   16 rectangles, 15 1/2" x 13", light blue
   12 rectangles, 15 1/2" x 13", medium blue faux suede
   9 rectangles, 15 1/2" x 13", dark blue
   4 rectangles, 15 1/2" x 13", blue floral
   8 rectangles, 15 1/2" x 13", off-white
   1 strip, 102 1/2" x 14", blue stripe
      (Piece three 14"-wide strips to achieve
      necessary length.)

Shams
   2 rectangles, 10" x 8", blue floral
   8 rectangles, 10" x 8", light blue
   8 rectangle, 10" x 8", medium blue faux suede
   4 strips, 3" x 22", blue stripe
   4 strips, 3" x 32", blue stripe
   4 rectangles, 27" x 22", blue solid

52

Instructions

Duvet Cover

Note: *Use ¹/₂" seam allowance unless otherwise specified.*

1. Place 15¹/₂" x 13" rectangles according to **Diagram 1**.

2. Sew rectangles in rows. Press seams to one side. Sew rows together and press seams to one side.

3. Sew 14"-wide blue stripe strip along top edge of pieced rectangles. (**Diagram 2**)

4. Fold raw edge of strip under ¹/₂". Fold strip in half covering seam allowance with folded edge. Sew along fold. (**Diagram 3**)

5. Place pieced top right sides together with king-size sheet. Be sure finished edge of sheet is even with top edge of pieced top. Trim sheet even with pieced top.

6. Sew along sides and bottom edge. Finish seam edges with small zigzag stitch.

7. Place velcro squares evenly spaced along top inside edges of front and back of duvet cover. Sew or fuse in place following manufacturer's directions.

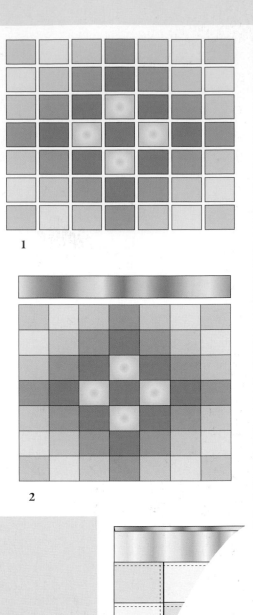

1

2

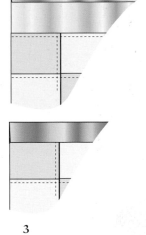

3

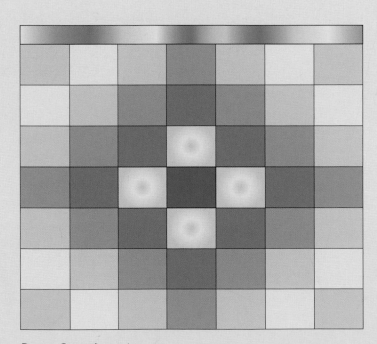

Duvet Cover Layout

Shams

1. Place 10" x 8" rectangles in three rows of three according to **Diagram 1**.

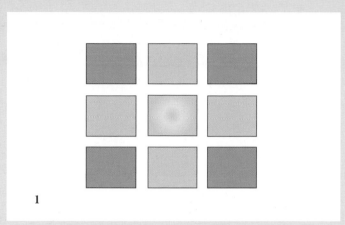

1

2. Sew rectangles in rows. Press seams to one side. Sew rows together. Press seams to one side.

3. Sew 3" x 22" blue stripe strips to opposite sides of pieced rectangles. Press seams to one side. Sew 3" x 32" blue stripe strips to top and bottom. Press seams to one side. (**Diagram 2**)

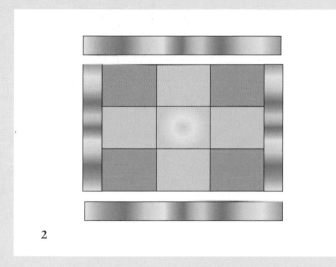

2

4. For blue solid backing rectangles, fold one 22" edge under ¼", then fold under another ½". Sew along first fold. (**Diagram 3**) Repeat for another backing rectangle.

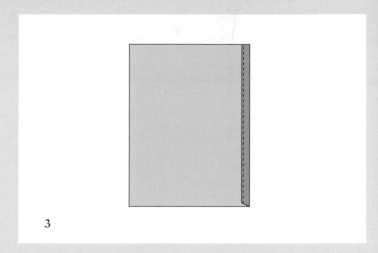

3

5. Place the two backing rectangles right sides together with pieced top, raw edges even and hemmed edges overlapping. (**Diagram 4**) Pin in place.

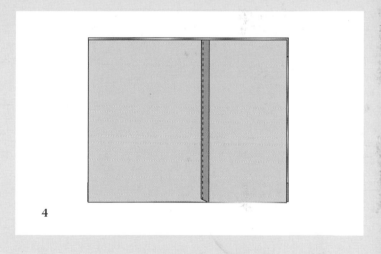

4

6. Sew along entire outer edge. (**Diagram 5**)

7. Turn sham right side out and press.

8. Sew sham front to back in the seam between pieced center and striped border to form a flange edge. (**Diagram 6**)

9. Repeat steps for second sham.

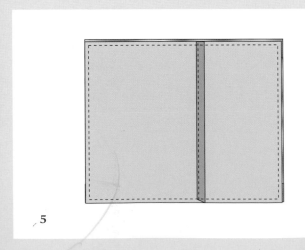

5

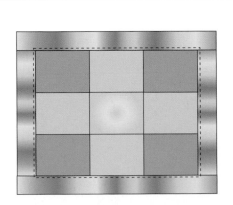

6

Four Patch Pillow

"Make a simple Four Patch Pillow into a conversation piece with a beaded trim."

time to make:
about 1 hour

Approximate Size: 12" square

Materials
fat quarter blue fabric
fat quarter white fabric
1¹/₂ yards beaded trim
12" pillow form

Cutting
2 squares, 7" x 7", blue
2 squares, 7" x 7", white
1 square, 13" x 13", white (backing)

Instructions

1. Sew a blue and white square together with right sides together using a $1/2$" seam allowance. Repeat. (**Diagram 1**)

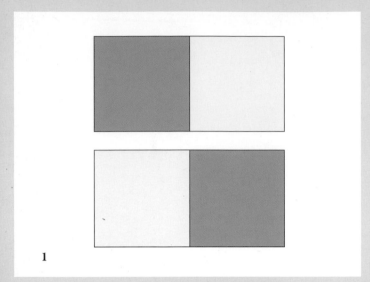

1

2. Sew pairs of squares together to form the pillow front. (**Diagram 2**)

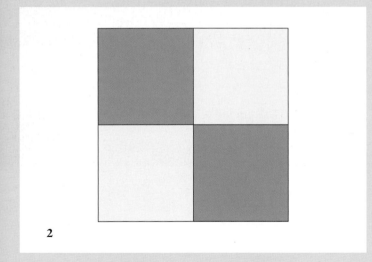

2

3. Place trim along outside edge of pillow front, then baste in place.

4. Place pillow front and back with right sides together; sew with a $1/2$" seam allowance leaving a 6" opening. (**Diagram 3**) Be careful not to catch trim in sewing.

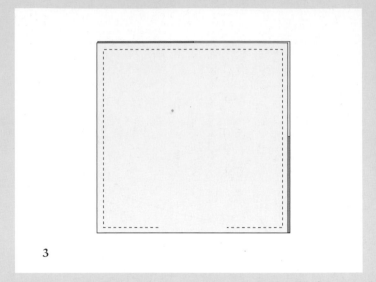

3

5. Turn pillow cover right side out. Check to see if any of the trim is caught in the stitching and fix if necessary.

6. Push pillow form through opening and then sew opening closed.

Neck Roll Pillow

Add the finishing touch to the bedroom with this pillow trimmed with wide ribbons.

time to make: about 1 hour

Approximate Size: 5" x 14"

Materials

3/8 yard white fabric

2/3 yard beaded trim, 1"-wide

2 yards ribbon, 1 1/2"-wide

5" x 14" neck roll pillow form

Cutting

1 rectangle, 12" x 24", white

Instructions

1. Fold short edge of white rectangle under ¼", then another ½"; press. Sew along first fold. (**Diagram 1**) Repeat on opposite side.

3. Fold white rectangle in half lengthwise with right sides together and raw edges even. Sew ½" from raw edges to form a tube. (**Diagram 3**) Machine zigzag along raw edge to finish. Turn right side out.

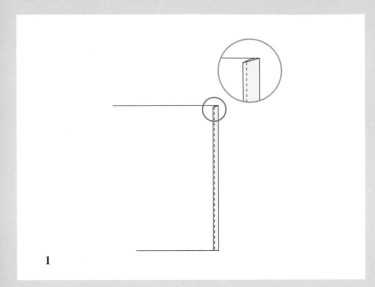

1

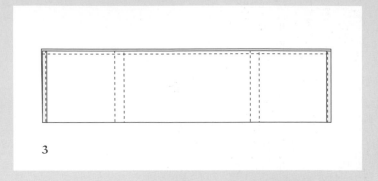

3

2. Measure 6" from hemmed side. Cut trim in two 12" lengths and place at that measurement and sew along both sides. Repeat on other side. (**Diagram 2**)

4. Center pillow form inside tube. Cut ribbon in half. Tie each end of tube with ribbon to complete pillow.

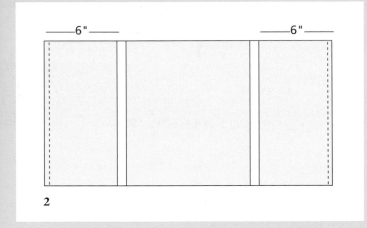

—— 6" —— —— 6" ——

2

Rosebud Pillow

An easy-to-make rosebud crowns this delightful round pillow.

time to make:
about 2 hours

Approximate Size: 12" round

Materials

1 yard yard floral print fabric
12" round pillow form
5 yards of string and a fabric marking pencil

Cutting

1 square, 24", floral print
1 strip, 6"-wide by width of fabic, floral print

Instructions

1. Fold floral print square in half with right sides together; fold again. **(Diagram 1)**

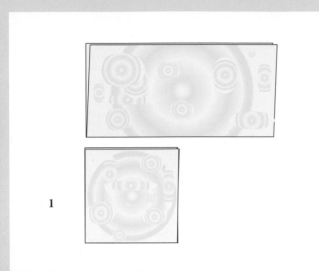

1

2. Tie a piece of string to pencil, then measure and cut string 12" long. **(Diagram 2)**

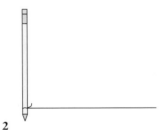

2

3. With folded square on a flat surface, position end of string at corner where folded ends meet. Hold pencil so string is taut and draw a line from corner to corner. **(Diagram 3)**

fold

fold

3

4. Keep square folded and cut along drawn line. When fabric is unfolded, you will have a circle. **(Diagram 4)**

5. Fold edge of circle 1/2" toward wrong side; baste in place. Set sewing machine to a zigzag stitch. Cut a piece of string the

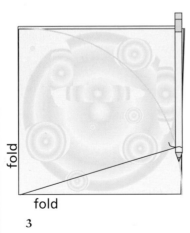

4

circumference of the circle plus 12" Place string along edge of circle with beginning of string dangling about 5" or 6". Machine zigzag over string being careful not to catch string in sewing. Continue sewing zigzag around entire circle; cut string leaving about 6" loose. **(Diagram 5)**

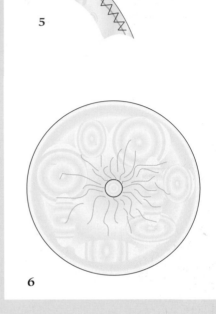

5

6. Place pillow form in center of wrong side of circle and pull string as tight as possible. Tie string ends together and cut ends. **(Diagram 6)**

6

7. Fold 6" strip in half lengthwise with wrong sides together. Cut a piece of string the width of the strip plus 6" and machine zigzag over string as in step 5. **(Diagram 7)**

7

8. Pull string and roll strip onto itself to form a rosette. **(Diagram 8)**

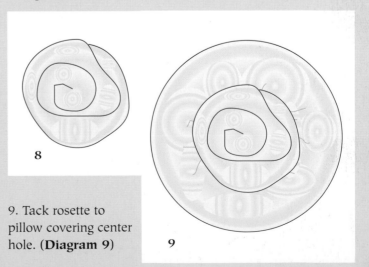

8

9. Tack rosette to pillow covering center hole. **(Diagram 9)**

9

Envelope Pillow

Different shaped pillows like this one decorated with fringe and a brooch add the perfect touch.

time to make: about 1 hour

Approximate Size: 16" x 16"

Materials
5/8 yard white fabric
2 yards trim
16" pillow form
optional: large decorative button or brooch

Cutting
2 squares, 17" x 17", white
2 rectangles, 9$\frac{1}{4}$" x 18$\frac{1}{2}$", white
1 strip, 2$\frac{1}{2}$" x 35", white

Instructions

1. Place 9¼" x 18½" rectangles right sides together. Find midpoint of one long edge. Draw diagonal line from the midpoint to each corner on opposite long edge. (**Diagram 1**)

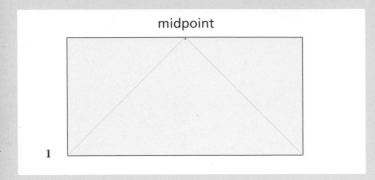

midpoint

1

2. Cut along diagonal lines.

3. Place trim between triangle layers along diagonal edges. Sew along diagonal ½" from edge being careful not to catch trim in sewing. (**Diagram 2**) Turn triangle right side out.

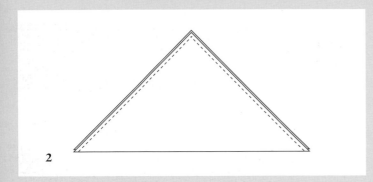

2

4. Place 17" x 17" white squares right sides together with trim in between along raw edges of three sides. Sew squares together along three sides using a ½" seam allowance. (**Diagram 3**) Turn right side out.

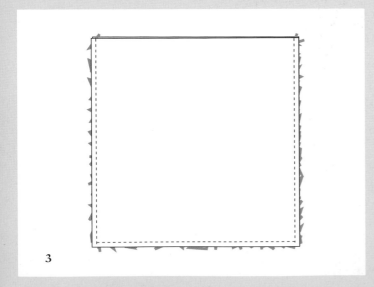

3

5. Place triangle right sides together with back square at opening; pin in place.

6. Fold the 2½" x 35" strip in half lengthwise with wrong sides together; press. Place along outside edge of entire opening with raw edges even; pin in place. Fold one short end of strip under ¼", then tuck other end inside and pin to opening. Sew with a ½" seam allowance being careful not to catch the front square in the stitching. (**Diagram 4**)

7. Fold strip down over seam allowance and hand stitch along folded edge. (**Diagram 5**)

8. Machine zigzag along raw edges of square.

9. Place pillow form inside rectangle and fold triangle over front.

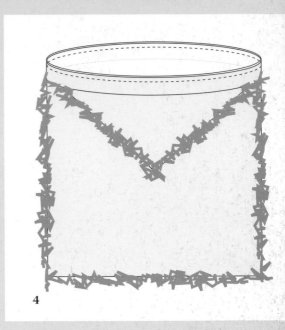

4

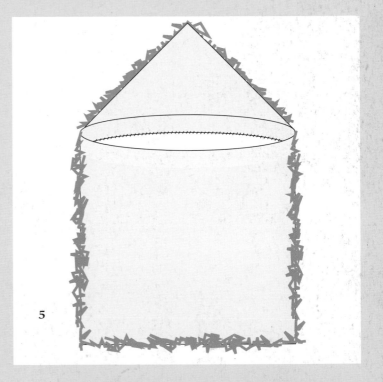

5

10. *Optional:* Sew button to rectangle front. Sew buttonhole to lower point of triangle matching size of button. Or, pin a brooch at lower corner of triangle onto front.

Fringed Pillow

Just trim a simple
rectangle with fringe,
and you have made
an elegant pillow.

time to make:
about 1 hour

Approximate Size: 12" x 16" (without flange)

Materials
1 yard medium blue fabric
1³/4 yards trim
12" x 16" pillow form
removable fabric marking pen or pencil

Cutting
1 rectangle, 17" x 21", medium blue
2 rectangles, 17" x 15", medium blue

Instructions

1. Fold one 17" edge of a 17" x 15" rectangle under ¼" then fold another ¼". Stitch along first fold. (**Diagram 1**) Repeat on remaining 17" x 15" rectangle.

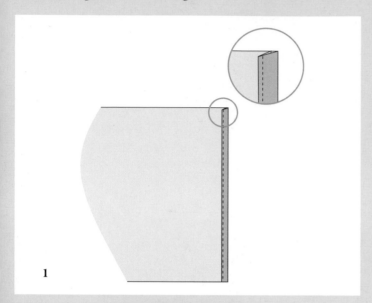

1

2. Place the two hemmed rectangles right sides together with the 17" x 21" rectangle; the hemmed edges should overlap. (**Diagram 2**)

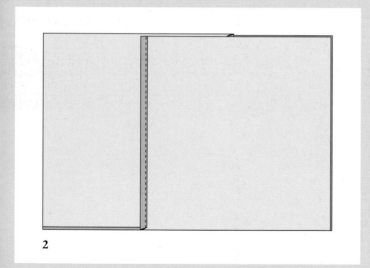

2

3. Sew along all four sides using a ½" seam allowance. (**Diagram 3**)

4. Zigzag along raw edges of seams and turn right side out. Press.

5. Draw lines 2" from each edge of sewn rectangle. (**Diagram 4**).

6. Sew along drawn lines to form a flange. (**Diagram 5**)

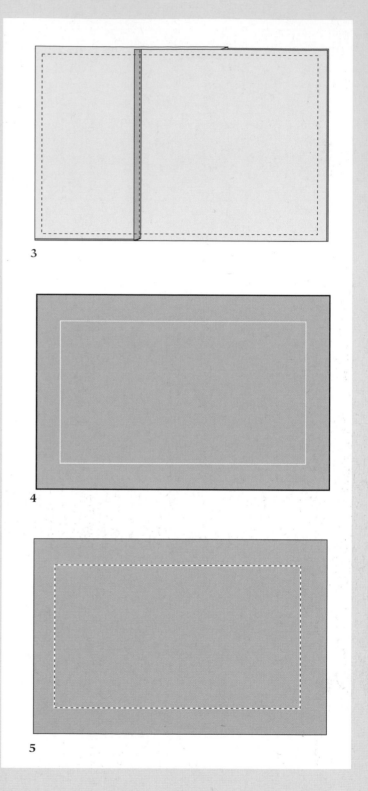

3

4

5

7. Place trim on just-stitched line and sew in place.

8. Place pillow form inside pillow cover to finish.

For Christmas

It's time for Christmas and between all the shopping and baking, make some time to create these wonderful projects that will enhance your Christmas decorating.

A group of elegant ornaments created from velvet and brocade will truly trim your tree.

How about making a velvet tree skirt and a matching stocking big enough for all your Yuletide gifts.

Make the house even more seasonal by using the velvet to create a Yuletide table runner that is decorated with gold tassels and gold bows.

And finally, make a Golden Bowl, which can hold a display of ornaments, holly and Christmas cards.

Now you are really ready for Christmas.

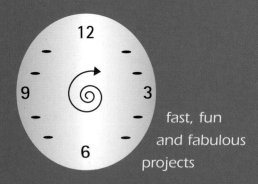

fast, fun and fabulous projects

Elegant Ornaments

"...elegant ornaments created from velvet and brocade will truly trim your tree."

time to make: about 2 hours

Approximate Size: 8" long

Materials
fat quarter dark green velvet
fat quarter burgundy velvet
fat quarter gold brocade
1 1/2 yards gold ribbon
1/2 yard burgundy ribbon
tracing paper or template plastic
polyester stuffing

Patterns
Note: *Trace Patterns onto tracing paper or template plastic. Cut out along drawn lines.*
Angel (page 70)
Star (page 71)
Tree (page 72)
Stocking (page 73)

Cutting
Note: *Place fabric right sides together, then cut out pattern shapes.*
2 Angels, gold brocade
2 Stars, gold brocade
2 Trees, dark green velvet
2 Stockings, burgundy velvet

68

Instructions

1. Place velvet or brocade shapes right sides together. Sew along entire shape leaving a 2" opening for turning. **(Diagram 1)**

2. Turn ornament right side out through opening.

3. Stuff ornaments with polyester stuffing, then stitch opening closed

4. Refer to photographs and add ribbons. Cut 12" pieces of ribbon and tie into bows. Attach to ornaments at center top. Form a loop with 6" of ribbon and attach behind bow.

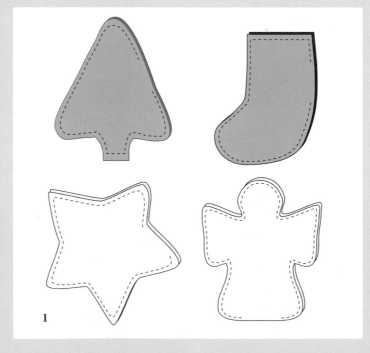

1

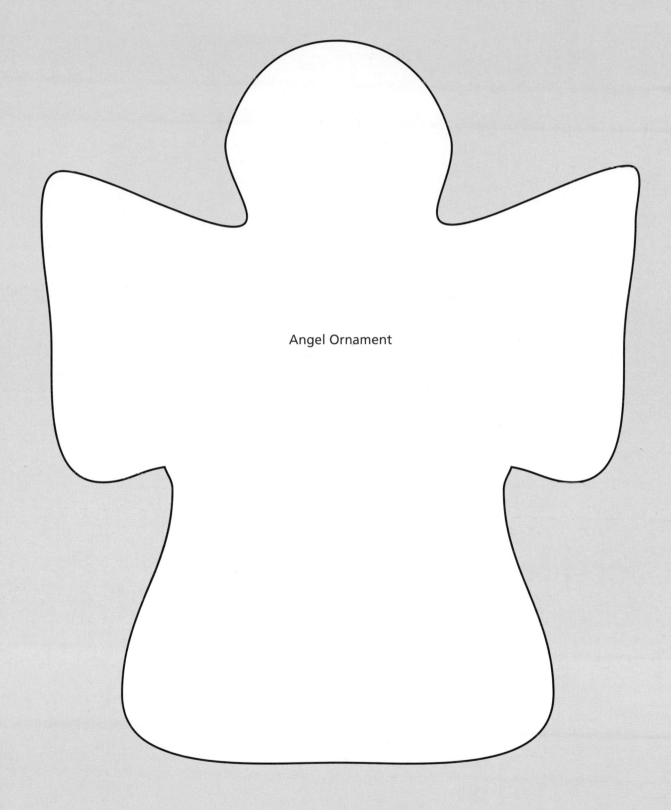

Angel Ornament

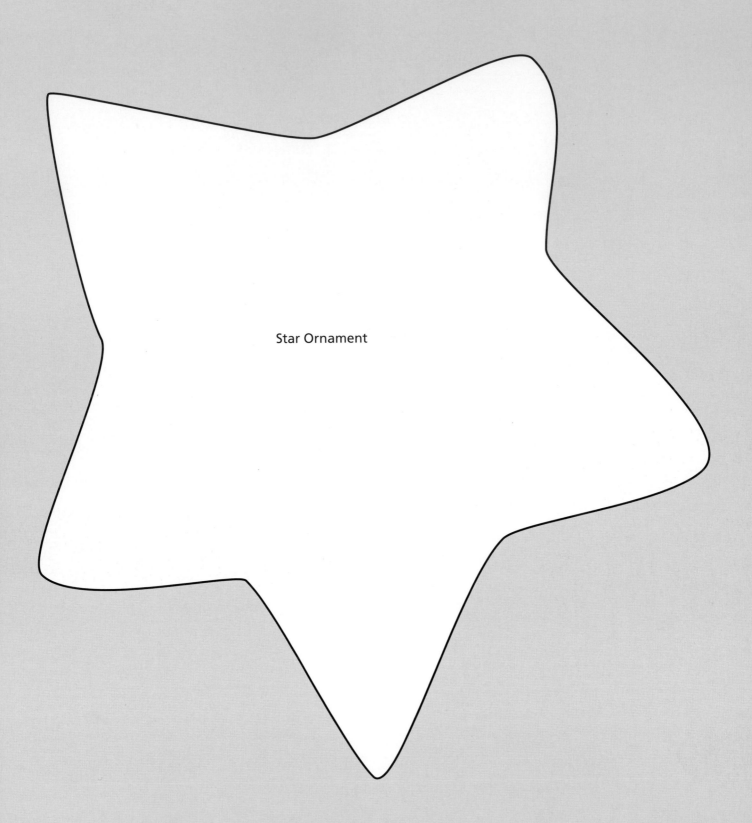

Star Ornament

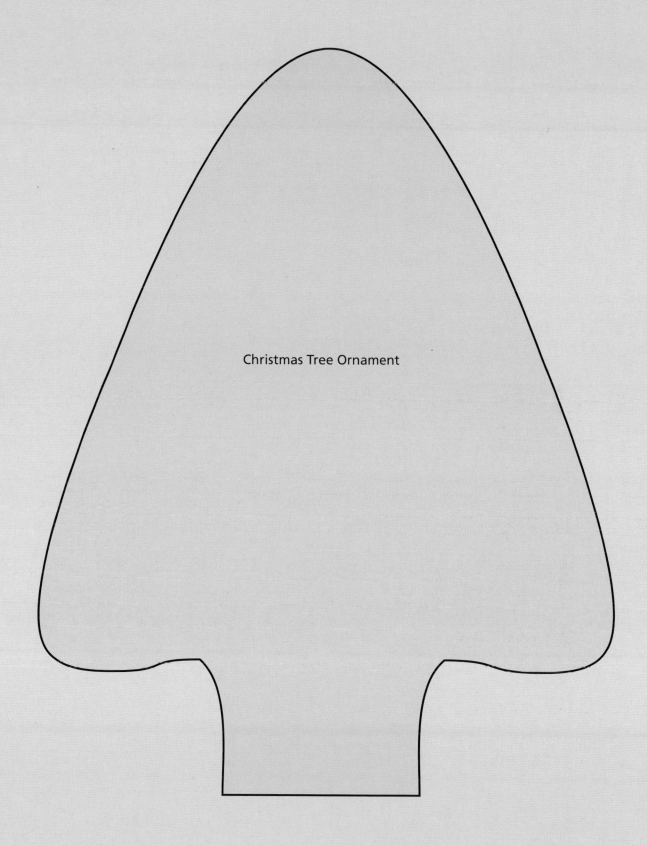

Christmas Tree Ornament

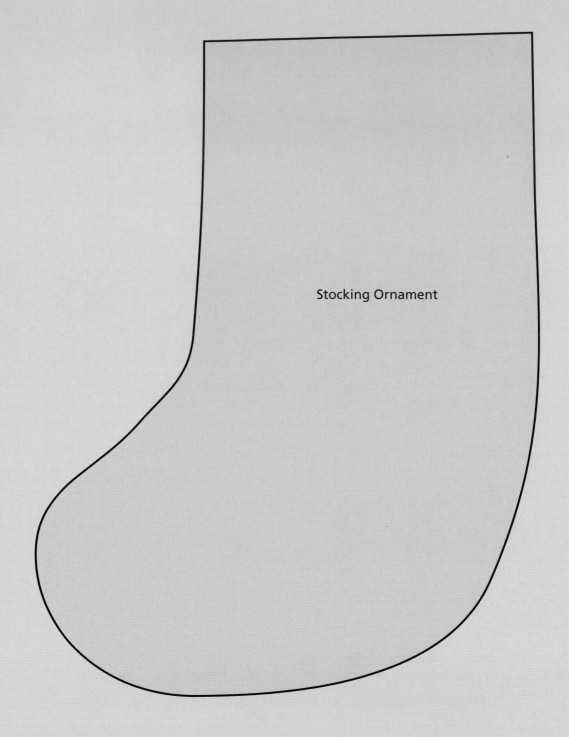

Stocking Ornament

Golden Bowl

Make a Golden Bowl to
hold a display of
ornaments, holly and
Christmas cards.

time to make:
about 1 hour

Approximate Size: 9" x 9"

Materials
fat quarter each outside fabric and inside fabric
12" square Fast-2-Fuse™ heavyweight fusible interfacing
    or Timtex™ heavyweight interfacing plus 5/8 yard
    paper-backed fusible web
matching thread
1 sheet template plastic
permanent marker
removable fabric pen or pencil

Pattern
Golden Bowl (page 77)

Instructions

1. Trace pattern onto template plastic using permanent marker. Turn template plastic and trace other half of pattern. Cut out template along drawn line. Trace and cut center circle template in same manner. (**Diagram 1**)

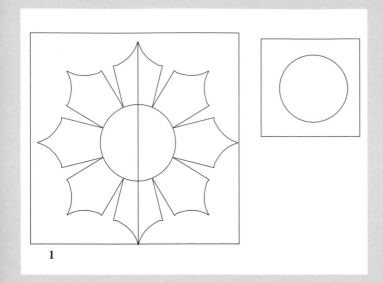

1

2. If using Timtex™, cut two squares larger than the outer dimension of the pattern from paper-backed fusible web. Fuse onto wrong side of outside and inside fat quarters. **Note**: *If using fabric with metallic gold, use a press cloth when fusing.*

3. Cut a square from Timtex™ the same measurements as the fused fabric from step 2. Remove paper backing and fuse fabric squares to each side of Timtex™ to form a three-layer unit.

4. If using Fast-2-Fuse™, cut two fabric squares from fabric and one from the Fast-2-Fuse™. Following manufacturer's directions, fuse fabric to both sides of Fast-2-Fuse™.

5. Place template on top of three-layer unit and trace using a removable fabric pen or pencil. (**Diagram 2**) Cut out along drawn line.

6. Place circle template in center of bowl layers on inside fabric and trace. (**Diagram 3**)

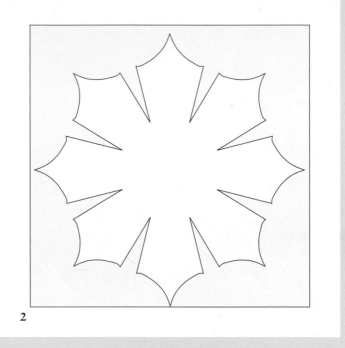

2

3

7. Place unit under sewing machine needle. Set machine to a tight zigzag or satin stitch and sew slits. Begin sewing at inside point and sew toward outside edge butting up the edges as you sew. (**Diagram 4**) Repeat for all slits. This gives the bowl shape.

8. Form the base of the bowl by sewing satin stitches along drawn circle.

9. Satin stitch around entire outer edge of bowl to finish.

4

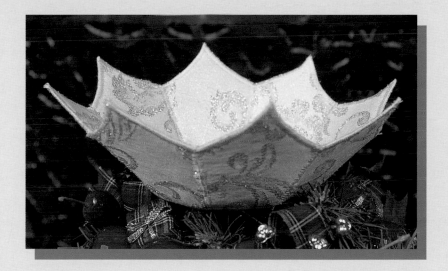

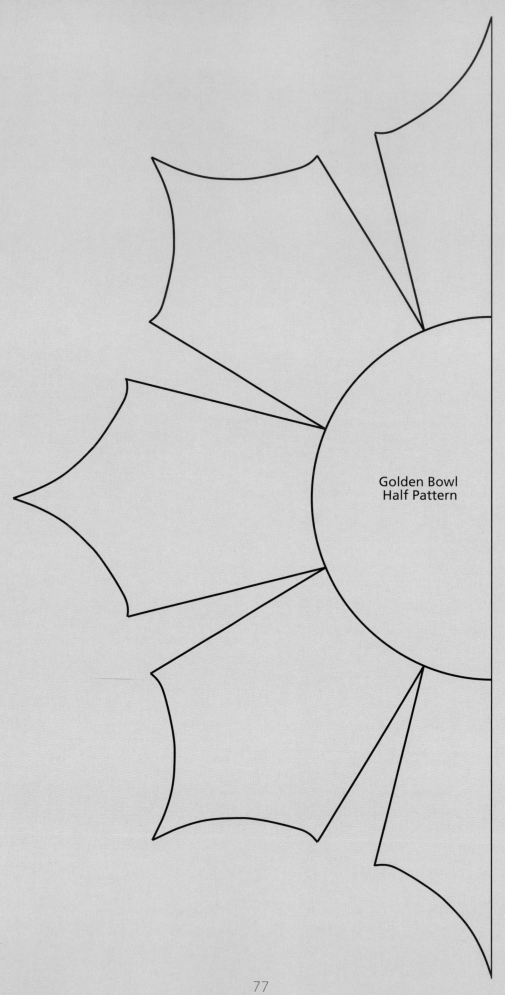

Golden Bowl
Half Pattern

Velvet Tree Skirt

What could be more elegant than a tree skirt made of velvet and trimmed in gold?

time to make: about 6 hours

Approximate Size: 49" at widest width

Materials
1 yard burgundy velvet
1¹/2 yards dark green velvet (includes backing)
thick batting
12 yards gold ribbon
16 gold tassels (2" long)
fabric marker
quilting thread

Cutting
Note: *Read Working with Velvet, page 131, before beginning.*
16 squares, 8" x 8", burgundy velvet
9 squares, 8" x 8", dark green velvet
1 square, 40" x 40", backing
1 square, 40" x 40", batting

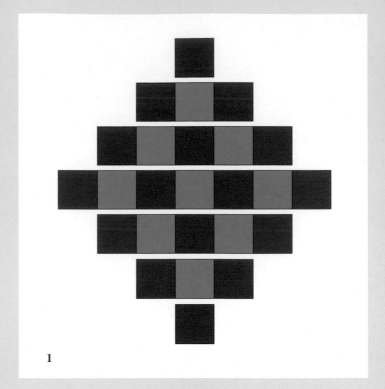

1

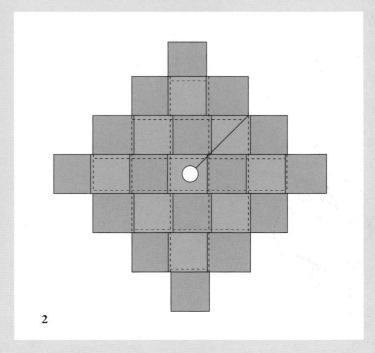

2

Instructions

Note: *Use a 1/2" seam allowance throughout.*

1. Sew burgundy and dark green velvet squares together in rows. (**Diagram 1**) Sew rows together.

2. Turn sewn squares over so wrong side is up. Draw a 4" circle in the center dark green square. Draw a line from the drawn circle and diagonally through an adjacent dark green square. (**Diagram 2**) **Hint:** *Use a glass or small bowl. The circle can be slightly smaller or larger than 4".*

3. Place batting square on flat surface, then place backing square right side up on batting. Center the sewn squares right side down on backing. Pin layers in place.

4. Sew along entire outside edge of sewn squares using a 1/2" seam allowance. (**Diagram 3**)

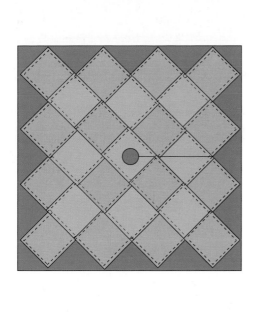

3

6. Cut along drawn straight line through all layers. (**Diagram 5**)

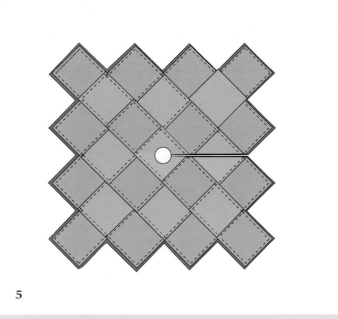

5

5. Trim batting and backing even with skirt top. (**Diagram 4**) Cut off outside points and clip inner points.

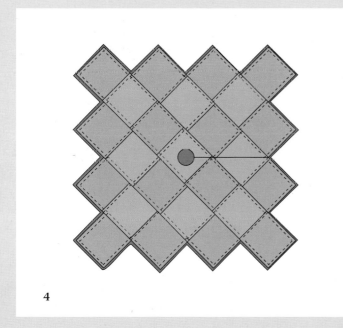

4

7. Sew along one cut edge, then continue sewing 1/2" from drawn circle. (**Diagram 6**) Leave other side open for turning.

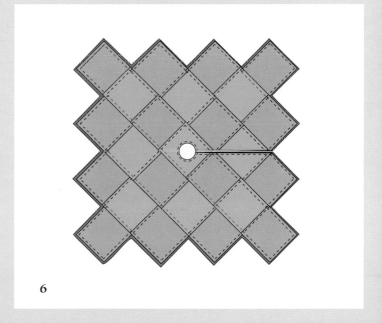

6

8. Turn right side out through side opening. Hand stitch opening closed.

9. Cut ribbon into 18" lengths and make 22 bows. You will have two 18" lengths remaining. Tack layers together at corners using quilting thread, then tack a bow at each corner to cover previous stitches.

10. Sew a remaining length of gold ribbon on each end of circle opening. Attach a tassel at each outer point.
(Diagram 7)

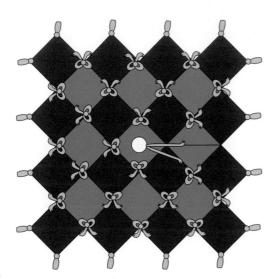

7

81

Yuletide Table Runner

How about making a table runner to match your velvet tree skirt?

time to make: about 3 hours

Approximate Size: 14" x 42"

Materials
3/8 yard burgundy velvet
1/4 yard dark green velvet
1/2 yard backing
thin batting *(optional)*
16 gold tassels (1" long)
3 yards gold ribbon

Cutting
Note: *Read Working with Velvet, page 131, before beginning.*
12 squares, 6" x 6", burgundy velvet
5 squares, 6" x 6", dark green velvet
1 rectangle, 15" x 43", backing
1 rectangle, 15" x 43", batting *(optional)*

Instructions.

Note: *Use ¹/₂" seam allowance.*

1. Sew burgundy and dark green squares together in rows. **(Diagram 1)**

1

2. Sew rows together. **(Diagram 2)**

2

3. If using batting, place on flat surface. Place backing on top of batting with right side up.

4. Place table runner top right side down on top of backing rectangle. Pin in place. Sew along outside edge of top leaving one short end unstitched. **(Diagram 3)**

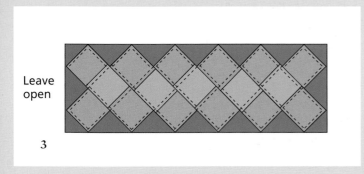

Leave open

3

5. Trim batting and backing even with top. Cut off outside points, and clip inner points. **(Diagram 4)**

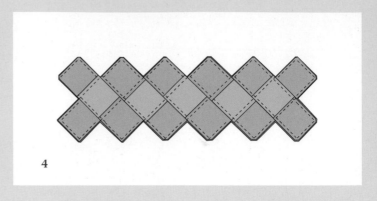

4

6. Turn right side out through opening. Sew opening closed.

7. Cut 18" lengths of gold ribbon and make six bows. Tack layers together at corners using quilting thread, then tack a bow at each corner to cover previous stitches. Attach a small tassel at each outer point. **(Diagram 5)**

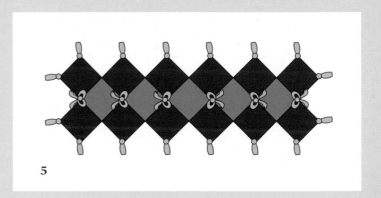

5

Royal Stocking

Make a stocking to match your tree skirt and table runner that is "big enough for all your Yuletide gifts."

time to make:
about 3 to 4 hours

Approximate Size: 18" long

Materials

1/2 yard burgundy velvet
1/4 yard dark green velvet
1/2 yard Christmas print (lining)
1/4 yard gold brocade
tracing paper or template plastic
ruler

Cutting

Note: *Read Working with Velvet, page 131, before beginning.*

16 squares, 4" x 4", dark green velvet
13 squares, 4" x 4", burgundy velvet
1 Stocking, burgundy velvet (back)
2 Stockings, Christmas print (lining)
1 rectangle, 5 1/2" x 23", gold brocade (stocking cuffs)
1 rectangle, 5 1/2" x 23", Christmas print
   (stocking cuffs lining)

Patterns

Stocking Lower Toe (page 86)
Stocking Upper Toe (page 87)

Instructions

Note: *Use 1/2" seam allowance.*

1. For Stocking front, sew burgundy and dark green squares together in rows. **(Diagram 1)**

2. Sew rows together. **(Diagram 2)**

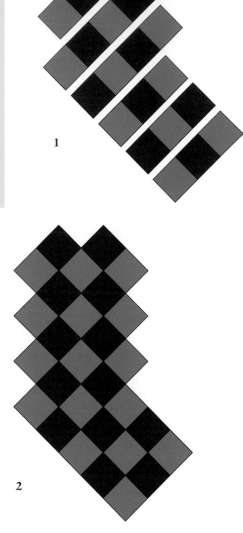

3. Place pieced squares right sides together with burgundy velvet stocking. With burgundy velvet stocking on top, sew 1/2" from all edges except top edge. **(Diagram 3)**

4. Trim pieced squares even with stocking back. Turn right side out.

5. Sew Stocking linings right sides together along all edges except top edge. **(Diagram 4)**

6. Place lining inside velvet stocking with wrong sides together. Line up top raw edges.

7. Place Cuff and Cuff lining with right sides together. Sew along both short sides and one long side. **(Diagram 5)**

8. Clip corners and turn Cuff right side out. Press carefully.

9. Starting with end of Cuff even with heel end of stocking, place Cuff inside Stocking next to lining with raw edges even. **(Diagram 6)** Sew along raw edges. Turn cuff over toward outside of stocking.

10. Fold Cuff to outside of Stocking to complete.

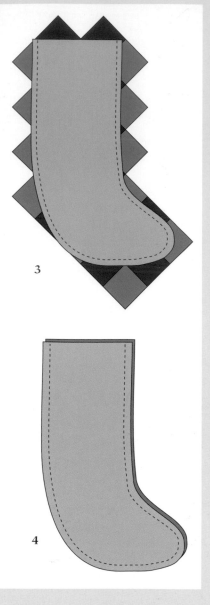

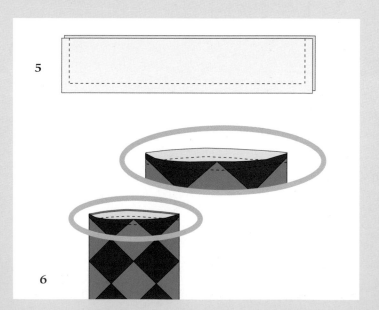

Pattern

Note: *To make Stocking pattern, trace Stocking
Lower Toe pattern onto tracing paper or template
plastic. Place Stocking Upper Toe next to Lower
Toe along line noted on pattern and continue
tracing until you have lower curved portion of
Stocking. Using a ruler, draw straight lines
extending 12" above Upper Toe; connect lines
across top. Cut out Stocking along outer
drawn lines.* (**Diagram A**, *page 87*)

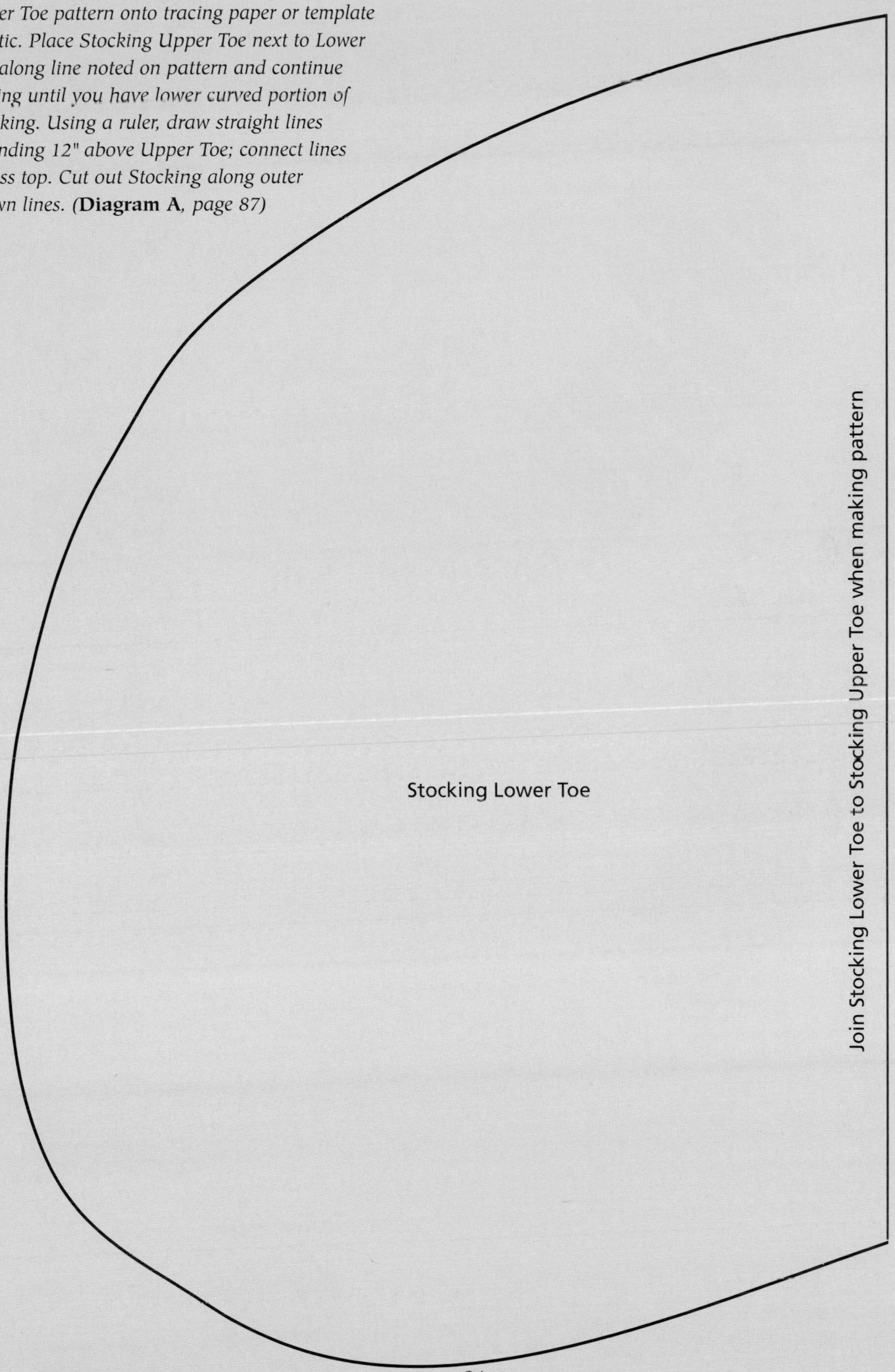

Stocking Lower Toe

Join Stocking Lower Toe to Stocking Upper Toe when making pattern

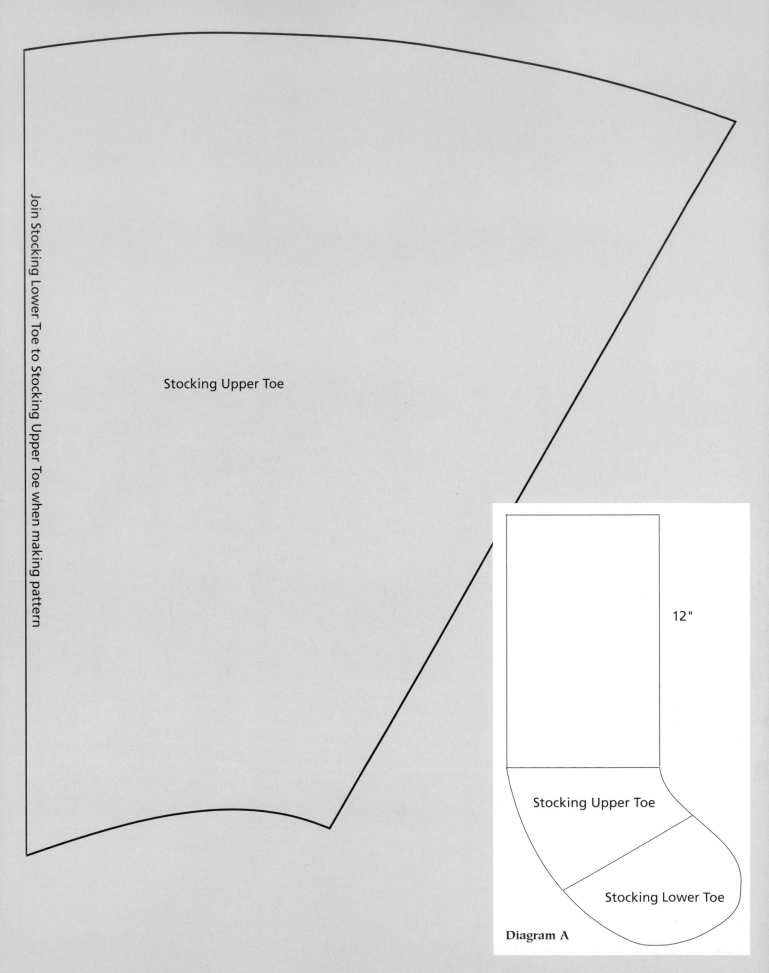

Join Stocking Lower Toe to Stocking Upper Toe when making pattern

Stocking Upper Toe

12"

Stocking Upper Toe

Stocking Lower Toe

Diagram A

terrific tote grab bag suede evening purse make a doggy happy magic jacket book covers quilt of cars yoyo vest terrific tote grab b

For Gift Giving

There always seems to be a time for gift giving whether it's a birthday, Christmas, a graduation, or just a time to say, "I'm thinking of you."

Make a Terrific Tote for a friend to carry all of her goodies. If she's a special friend, add the matching Grab Bag Purse complete with the cosmetic pouch and eyeglass case.

Take a plain sweatshirt and turn it into a Magic Jacket by cutting the sweatshirt and adding strips of fabric. What a great gift that would make! Use pre-made yoyos to create a one-of-a-kind vest for a favorite person.

For the person who loves to read, make some book covers; for the elegant Miss, a suede evening bag. If you find car fabric, you should certainly make the Quilt of Cars for a car fanatic (or you can make the quilt with other favorite fabrics).

And, don't forget the loyal family dog. She certainly deserves her very own bed and toys!

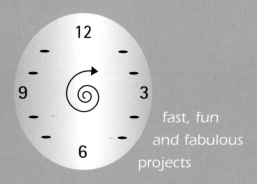

fast, fun
and fabulous
projects

Terrific Tote

Make this tote for a friend to carry all her goodies whether it's her birthday, Christmas, a graduation or just time to say, "I'm thinking of you."

time to make:
about 5 hours

Approximate Size: 19" x 16"

Materials

1 1/2 yards blue floral print fabric (tote)
1 1/2 yards blue fabric (lining)
3/8 yard border print fabric (outer pocket)
craft size fusible batting
1/2 yard lightweight fusible interfacing
5" x 13" piece of thin cardboard
removable fabric marking pen or pencil
matching thread

Cutting

2 rectangle 20" x 21", blue floral print
   (tote front and back)
2 squares, 20" x 20", blue (lining, tote front and back)
1 rectangle, 20" x 12", border print (outside pocket)
1 rectangle, 20" x 11", blue (lining for outside pocket)
2 rectangles, 20" x 28", blue floral print (inside pockets)
*2 strips, 3" x 64", blue floral print (handles)
2 squares, 20" x 20", fusible batting (tote front and back)
1 rectangle, 20" x 11", fusible batting (outside pocket)
2 rectangles 20" x 14", fusible batting (inside pockets)
2 strips, 3" x 64", lightweight fusible interfacing (handles)
2 rectangles, 6" x 14", blue (bottom)
*Cut two 3"-wide strips across the width of the fabric, then
sew together and cut to 64" long.

Instructions

1. For Tote front, place a 20" x 21" blue floral print square and 20" x 20" blue lining square wrong sides together with a 20" x 20" fusible batting square in between. The blue floral rectangle will extend 1" beyond the top edge of the layer and batting squares. (**Diagram 1**) Fuse layers together.

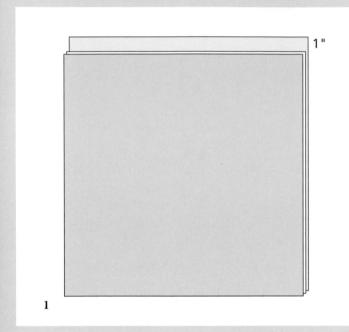

1

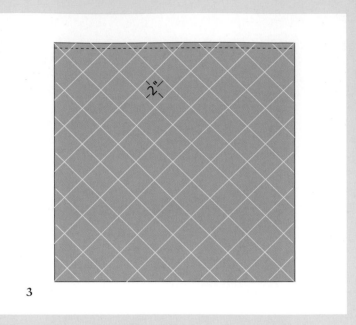

3

4. Repeat steps 1 and 2 for Tote back.

5. For outside pocket, place 20" x 12" border print rectangle and 20" x 11" blue lining rectangle wrong sides together with 20" x 11" batting in between. Top edge of border print rectangle will extend 1" beyond edge of lining and batting rectangles. (**Diagram 4**) Fuse layers together.

2. Fold extended blue floral edge under 1/2", then another 1/2" to form a hem. Stitch along first fold. (**Diagram 2**)

4

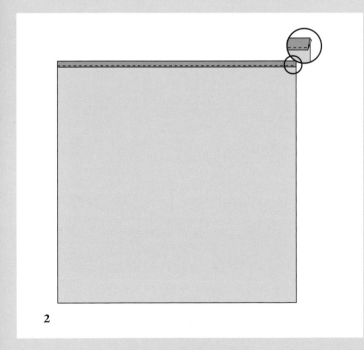

2

6. Fold extended border print edge under 1/4" then another 1/2" to form a hem. Stitch along first fold. (**Diagram 5**)

3. Draw diagonal lines about 2" apart, then sew along lines to hold the layers together. (**Diagram 3**) Use a longer stitch length (about 8 to 10 stitches per inch).

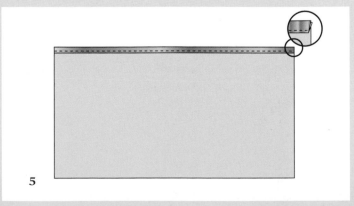

5

7. Pin pocket to lower end of Tote front matching raw edges. (**Diagram 6**)

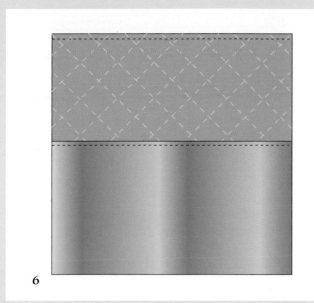

6

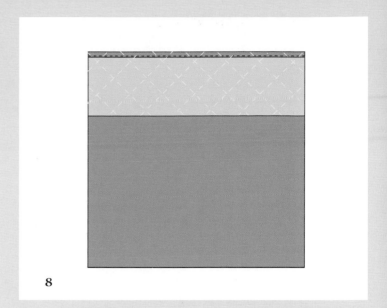

8

8. For inside pocket, fold 20" x 28" blue floral rectangle in half wrong sides together; place the 20" x 14" batting rectangle in between. (**Diagram 7**) Fuse layers together. Repeat for another pocket.

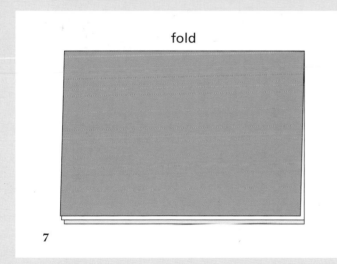

fold

7

9. Pin inside pockets to lower end of Tote front and Tote back. (**Diagram 8**)

10. For handles, fuse 3" x 64" interfacing strip to wrong side of 3" x 64" blue floral strip. Fold strip in half lengthwise with wrong sides together. Sew along long edge using a 1/4" seam allowance. Turn strip right side out and press. Repeat for remaining handle.

11. Measure 6" from each side edge of Tote front. Pin handle to Tote front along 6" mark on left side starting at bottom, going along 6" mark on right side and ending on bottom edge. (**Diagram 9**)

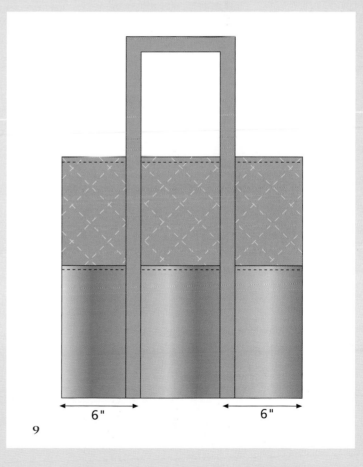

6"   6"

9

12. Beginning at one end of handle, topstitch close to edge along entire length; repeat along other edge. (**Diagram 10**)

92

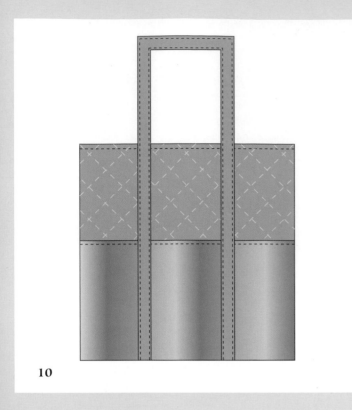

10

15. To form a flat bottom, fold lower corner so side seam and bottom edge seam match and a triangle is formed. (**Diagram 12**)

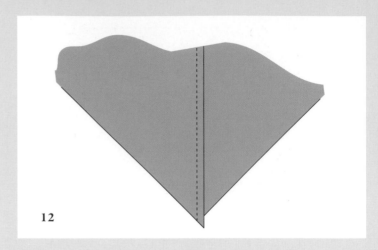

12

13. Repeat steps 10 to 12 for remaining handle on Tote back.

Note: *Sewing the handles to Tote front and back forms the outside and inside pockets.*

14. Place Tote front and tote back right sides together. Sew along side and bottom edges using a $1/2$" seam allowance. (**Diagram 11**) Sew again along first stitching to reinforce. Machine zigzag along seam allowances to finish edges.

16. Measure up about $3^1/2$" from point of triangle and sew across. (**Diagram 13**)

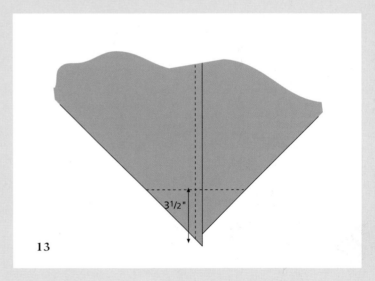

$3^1/2$"

13

17. Repeat steps 15 and 16 for other corner.

18. For Tote bottom, place the two 6" x 14" blue rectangles right sides together. Sew along one short side and both long sides using a $1/4$" seam allowance. Turn right side out. Place the 5" x 13" cardboard rectangle inside sewn rectangles. Fold raw edges in and hand stitch closed. Place cardboard rectangle in bottom of Tote.

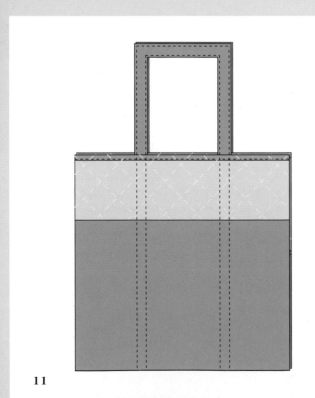

11

Grab Bag Purse

For a special friend make "the matching Grab Bag Purse complete with the Cosmetic Pouch and Eyeglass Case."

time to make: about 3 to 4 hours

Purse

Approximate Size: 14" x 12"

Materials

5/8 yard blue floral print
1 yard blue fabric (lining)
5/8 yard border print or contrasting print
1 yard Fast-2-Fuse™ heavyweight fusible interfacing
5/8 yard lightweight fusible interfacing
1/2 yard paper-backed fusible web
purchased purse handles
14" zipper

Cutting

2 rectangles, 14" x 17", blue floral print
   (Purse front and back)
4 squares, 5" x 5", blue floral print (handle tabs)
2 rectangles, 13" x 17", blue (lining)
2 strips, 5" x 16", blue (lining)
2 rectangles, 17" x 18", blue (inside pockets)
1 strip, 5 1/2" x 18", border print or contrasting print
   (outside pocket)

Optional:

2 strips each, 2 1/2" x 17", border print or contrasting print
   and paper-backed fusible web (top edge border)
2 rectangles, 13" x 17" fast-to-fuse
   (Purse front and back)
1 strip, 5 1/2" x 18", fusible interfacing (outside pocket)
2 rectangles, 17" x 18", fusible interfacing (inside pockets)

Instructions

1. For Purse front, following manufacturer's directions, iron 13" x 17" blue lining to 13" x 17" Fast-2-Fuse™; repeat. Iron 14" x 17" blue floral rectangle to opposite side; blue floral fabric will extend 1" past one end. **(Diagram 1)**

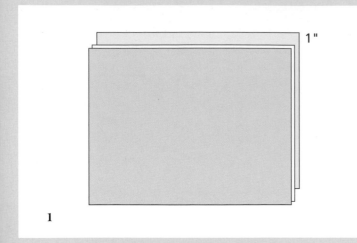

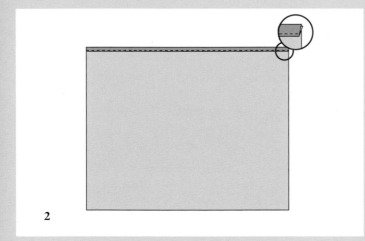

2. Fold extended end of fabric 1/2", then another 1/2". Sew along second fold. **(Diagram 2)**

3. Repeat steps 1 and 2 for Purse back.

Optional: *Fuse 2¹/2" x 17" border print strip to paper-backed fusible web following manufacturer's directions. Fuse to Purse front 3/4" from top edge. **(Diagram 3)** Use a machine satin stitch (tight zigzag) along raw edges of border print. Repeat for Purse back.*

4. For inside back pocket, follow manufacturer's instructions to fuse interfacing to wrong side of 13" x 17" blue lining rectangle. Fold in half with wrong sides together so piece is 8¹/2" x 17". **(Diagram 4)** Repeat for remaining pocket.

fold

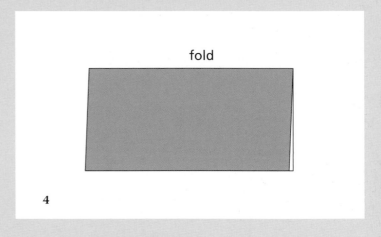

5. Pin or baste folded pockets to lining side of Purse back. **(Diagram 5)**

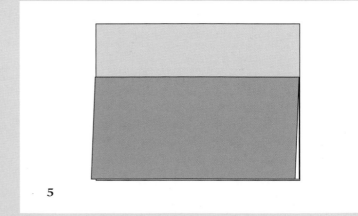

6. Sew down center of inside pocket through all layers for Purse back. (**Diagram 6**)

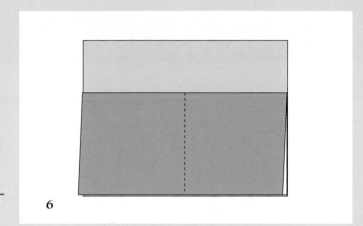

6

7. For inside front pocket, repeat steps 3 and 4.

8. For outside front pocket, follow manufacturer's directions to fuse interfacing to wrong side of 5 1/2" x 18" border print strip; fold in half crosswise. (**Diagram 7**)

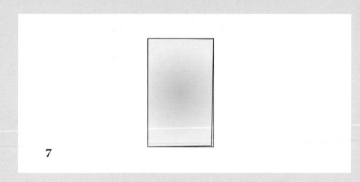

7

9. Place outside pocket centered on right side of Purse front with lower raw edges even. Sew along each side of outside pocket using a machine satin stitch. (**Diagram 8**) This will form three inside pockets on Purse Front.

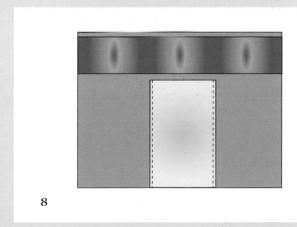

8

10. For the zipper top, fold 5" sides of both 5" x 16" blue strips under 1/4". Sew near fold. (**Diagram 9**)

9

11. Fold the 5" x 16" blue strip in half lengthwise with wrong sides together; press. Zigzag stitch along long raw edges of folded strip. (**Diagram 10**) Repeat for other strip.

10

12. Referring to manufacturer's instructions, sew zipper to folded edges of lining strips, making sure the zipper is centered along the length of the strips. (**Diagram 11**)

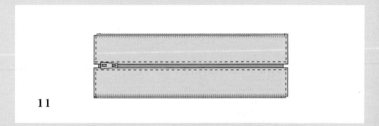

11

13. Place a long edge of the zipper strip about 3/4 " from top edge of Purse front with right side of zipper strip against lining side of Purse front. (**Diagram 12**) Pin in place.

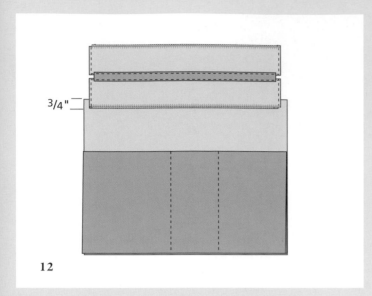

12

3/4"

14. Sew 1/4" from edge of zipper strip. (**Diagram 13**)

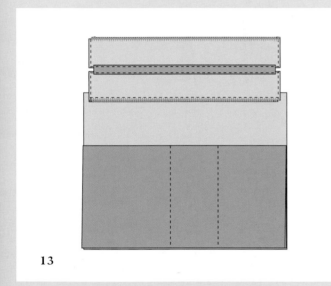

13

15. Repeat steps 11 and 12 on Purse back.

16. For the handle tabs, fold 5" blue floral print square in half with right sides together. Sew along long edge and one short edge using a 1/4" seam allowance. Turn tab right side out and press. Tuck open end in and stitch closed. Fold sewn tab in half lengthwise and stitch close to both long sides. (**Diagram 14**) Repeat for remaining three tabs.

14

18. For placement of tabs, center a purchased handle along top edge of Purse front. Mark each end of handle. Fold tabs in half, then pin tabs in place at marks on lining side of Purse front. (**Diagram 15**) Be sure zipper strip is facing down, away from top edge of Purse front.

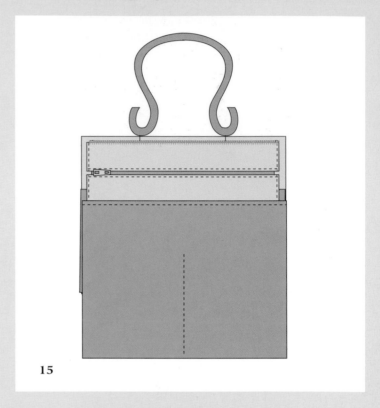

15

19. Sew in place along lower edge of tab, then again 1/4" from first stitching. (**Diagram 16**)

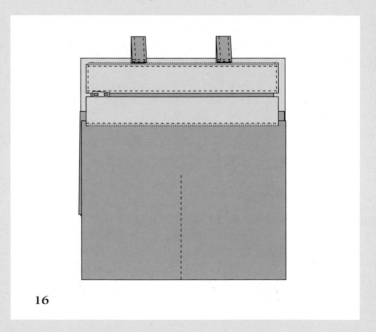

16

20. Repeat steps 18 and 19 for Purse back.

21. Place Purse front and back with right sides together. Sew along sides and lower edges using a 1/2" seam allowance. Sew again on top of previous stitching to reinforce. Finish edges using a machine satin stitch.

22. For lower corners, push lower corner to form a triangle so seam is in center. (**Diagram 17**)

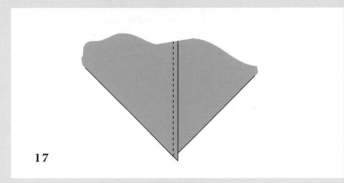

17

23. Sew a few stitches at each side of triangle, about 2" from lower point. (**Diagram 18**)

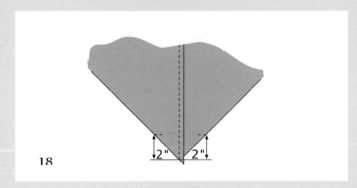

18

24. Repeat steps 22 and 23 on opposite corner.

25. Turn purse right side out and work corners to form a flat bottom for the purse.

26. Place handles through tabs and your new purse is ready to use.

Cosmetic Pouch

Approximate Size: 8" x 6"

Materials
fat quarter blue floral print fabric
fat quarter coordinating lining fabric
fusible batting
7" zipper

Cutting
2 rectangles each, 9" x 7", blue floral print, blue lining and batting
1 rectangle, 9" x 12", blue lining

Instructions

1. Place a blue floral print rectangle and a blue lining rectangle right sides together; place a batting rectangle underneath. Sew along one 9" edge using a 1/2" seam allowance. (**Diagram 1**) Repeat with remaining rectangles.

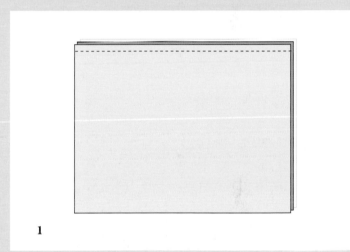

1

2. Trim batting close to seams. Turn fabric so both right sides are facing out with batting in between. Iron fabric layers to fuse batting.

3. Sew zipper along sewn edge of both layered rectangles with blue floral fabric facing out. (**Diagram 2**)

time to make:
about 1½ hours

4. For inside pocket, fold 9" x 12" blue lining rectangle with wrong sides together along 9" side so piece is 9" x 6"; press fold. (**Diagram 3**) Place folded rectangle in between quilted rectangles with fold at top edge and all raw edges even. Folded edge of rectangle will be about 1" below zipper. (**Diagram 4**)

3

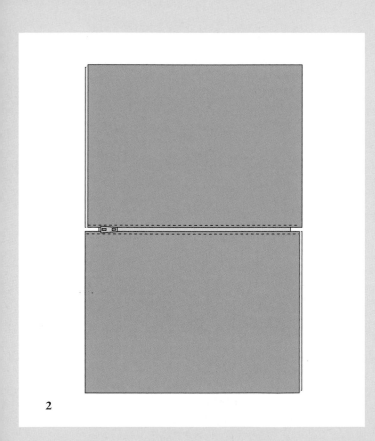

2

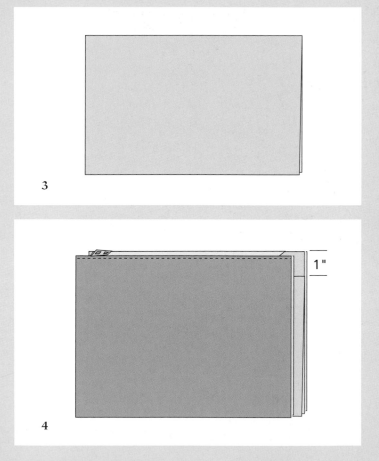

4

1"

5. Sew along raw edges with a $1/8$" seam allowance.
(**Diagram 5**) **Note:** *You are sewing with right side out.*

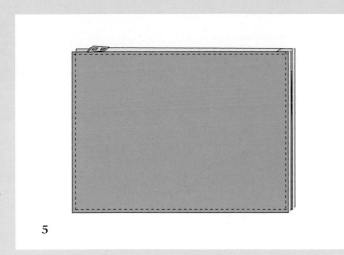

5

6. Open zipper and turn pouch wrong side out. Flatten out and press edges so they are as flat as possible. Sew along the sides and lower edge of pouch using a $1/4$" seam allowance to enclose raw edges of seam allowance just sewn.

7. Turn pouch right side out.

Eyeglass Case

Approximate Size: $31/2$" x 7"

Materials
fat quarter blue floral
scrap floral or border print (at least 5" x 9")
9" square fusible batting

Cutting
3 rectangles, 4" x 8", blue floral (back and lining)
1 rectangle, 4" x 8", border print (front)
2 rectangles, 4" x 8", batting

Instructions

1. For Eyeglass Case front, place border print and blue floral rectangles right sides together with batting rectangle underneath. Sew along top edge with a $1/4$" seam allowance. (**Diagram 1**)

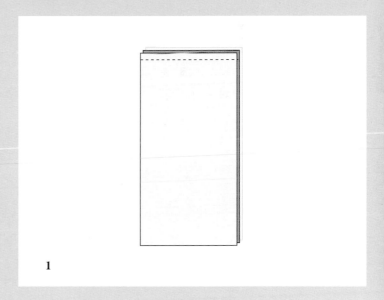

1

2. Repeat step 1 with the remaining two blue floral and batting rectangles.

time to make:
about 1 hour

3. Flip blue floral rectangle over seam so that batting is between the fabric rectangles. Press layers together to fuse. (**Diagram 2**) Topstitch 1/4" from sewn edge.

4. Place Eyeglass Case front and back with lining sides together. Sew along side and bottom edges using a 1/8" seam allowance. (**Diagram 3**)

2

3

5. Turn Case inside out; flatten seams and press. Sew again using a 1/4" seam allowance along sides and bottom edges to enclose seam.

Suede Evening Purse

"...for the elegant Miss, a suede evening purse."

time to make: about 3 hours

Approximate Size: 8" x 12"

Materials
1/4 yard black faux suede
1/4 yard lining fabric
1/4 yard fusible interfacing
no-sew black velcro dot (1/2" diameter)
white marking pencil

Cutting
2 rectangles each, 9" x 15", black faux suede and lining
(purse front and back, lining front and back)
2 rectangles, 10" x 8", lining (pockets)
2 strips, 2 1/2" x 21", black faux suede (handles)
2 strips, 2 1/2" x 21", fusible interfacing

Instructions

1. For purse front, place one 9" x 15" black faux suede rectangle on a flat surface. Using a ruler, draw a line with white marking pencil down center of right side of rectangle. (**Diagram 1**)

2. Draw four lines 1" apart on each side of center line. (**Diagram 2**)

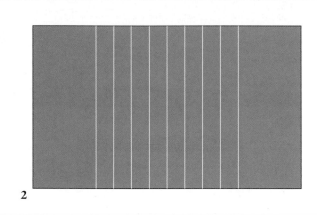

3. Fold rectangle along center drawn line wrong sides together. Sew using a ¹/4" seam allowance to within 2" from bottom of rectangle. (**Diagram 3**)

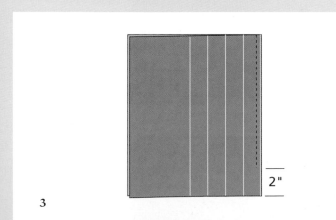

4. Fold along remaining lines and sew towards bottom, ending sewing 1" above previous line. (**Diagram 4**)

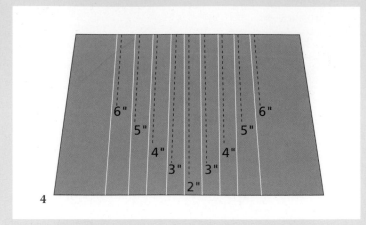

5. Place remaining black faux suede and lining rectangles on cutting mat. Place sewn black faux suede rectangle on top. Trim 9" x 15" black rectangle and both 9" x 15" lining rectangles even with sewn Purse front. (**Diagram 5**)

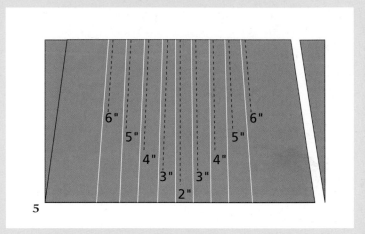

6. Place faux suede purse front and back right sides together. Sew along side and lower edges using a ¹/4" seam allowance. (**Diagram 6**) Turn purse right side out.

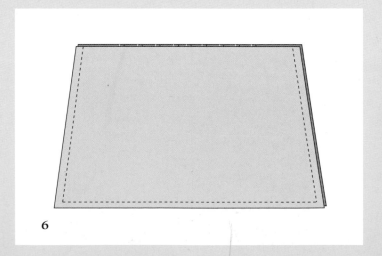

7. For inside pocket, fold 10" x 8" lining rectangle in half with right sides together; folded piece should measure 5" x 8". Sew along sides with a 1/4" seam allowance. **(Diagram 7)**

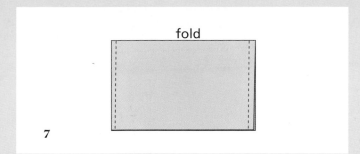

fold

7

8. Turn pocket right side out and press. Fold lower raw edges under 1/4" and press.

9. Center pocket on lining with folded side toward top edge about 1 1/2" from top. Sew along side and bottom edges close to edge of pocket. **(Diagram 8)**

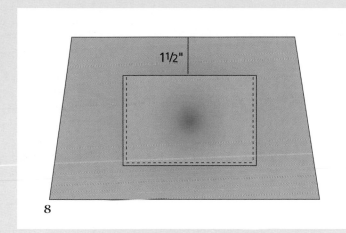

1 1/2"

8

10. Repeat steps 7 to 9 for remaining lining and pocket.

11. Place lining front and back with right sides together. Sew along side and lower edges using a 1/4" seam allowance. **(Diagram 9)**

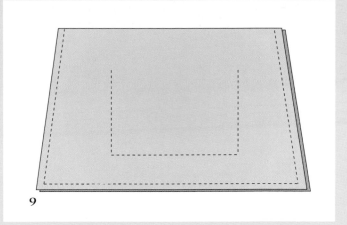

9

12. Fold top raw edges of purse and lining under 1/4"; press.

13. Place lining inside purse, matching folded top edges. Pin in place.

14. For handles, fuse interfacing to wrong side of faux suede strip following manufacturer's directions.

15. Fold strip in half lengthwise with right sides together. Sew along long raw edge with 1/4" seam allowance. Turn handle right side out and press lightly. Sew 1/4" from each side down length of strip. Repeat for remaining strip.

16. Measure 2" from each end of purse front. Position handle ends at the 2" mark in pin in place in between the purse and lining. **(Diagram 10)** Repeat for purse back.

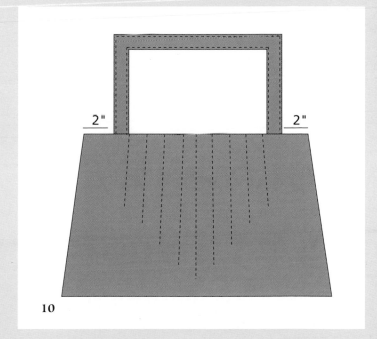

2"   2"

10

17. Sew near upper edge of purse catching handles in sewing. (**Diagram 11**)

18. Position sticky velcro dot at top center of purse front and back. Let set for 24 hours before using purse.

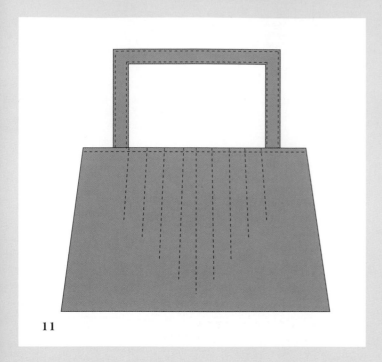

11

Make a Doggy Happy

And when making gifts, "don't forget the loyal family dog. She certainly deserves her very own bed and toys!"

time to make:
about 2 to 3 hours

Doggy Bed

Approximate Size: 16" x 21"

Materials
1¼ yard animal print flannel
½ yard brown flannel
12" x 72" extra-loft batting
paper plate (any size)
fabric marking pencil
zipper foot for your sewing machine

Cutting
1 rectangle, 17" x 22", animal print flannel
1 rectangle, 17" x 22", brown flannel
2 strips, 7"-wide by width of fabric, animal print flannel
2 or 3 rectangles, 17" x 22", extra-loft batting
1 strip, 12" x 72" strip, extra-loft batting

106

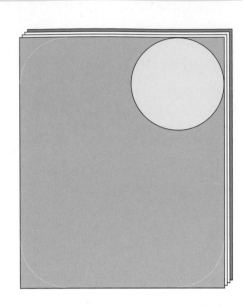

1

2

3

Instructions

Note: *Use a 1/2" seam allowance throughout unless noted otherwise.*

1. Layer animal print flannel rectangle wrong side up, then all 17" x 22" batting rectangles and finally brown flannel rectangle right side up. Pin layers together.

2. Place paper plate at corner and mark curved edge using fabric marking pencil. Repeat at remaining three corners. **(Diagram 1)**

3. Cut corners at marked lines. **(Diagram 2)**

4. Using a short, wide machine zigzag stitch, sew along all edges of layered rectangles. **(Diagram 3)**

5. Sew animal print flannel strips together along short edges. Press seam open and cut strip strip to 76". **(Diagram 4)**

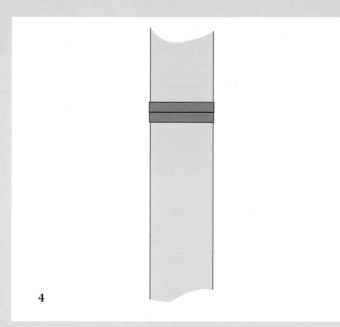

4

7. Take batting strip and roll to form a long tube. **(Diagram 5)**

5

8. Starting at one end of animal print flannel strip, place batting tube on wrong side of strip; fold flannel strip over batting matching raw edges. **(Diagram 6)** Pin in place.

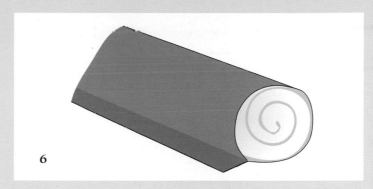

6

9. Continue folding and pinning flannel strip over entire length of batting tube. The flannel should extend about 4" past the batting.

10. Pin tube to layered flannel rectangle with animal print sides together.

11. Place zipper foot on your sewing machine. Begin sewing tube to rectangle about 6" from end of tube. Sew to about 6" from end of tube and backstitch.

12. Butt up the ends of batting tube and whipstitch ends closed.

Note: *If batting is too long, cut off end and then whipstitch closed.*

13. Fold extended flannel strip toward wrong side then cover ends of batting tube with flannel. Finish sewing tube to rectangle.

14. Machine zigzag along raw edges of seam allowance to finish edges.

15. Fold tube up over seam allowance and doggy bed is ready for use.

time to make:
about 30 to 60 minutes

Dog Bone Toy

Approximate Size: 11" long

Pattern
Dog Bone (page 110)

Materials
fat quarter flannel or fleece
polyester stuffing

Cutting
2 Dog Bones, flannel or fleece

Instructions

1. Place Dog Bone shapes right sides together. Sew using a 1/4" seam allowance; leave a 3" opening. (**Diagram 1**)

2. Turn Dog Bone right side out through opening. Fill with polyester stuffing.

3. Whipstitch opening closed.

1

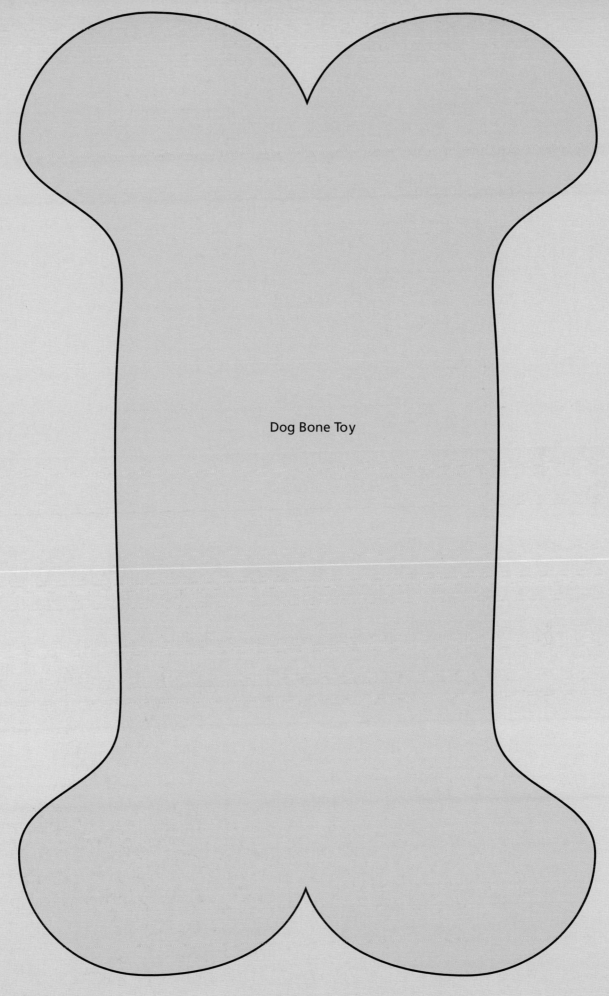

Dog Bone Toy

time to make:
about 1 hour

Ice Cream Cone Toy

My spoiled little pug, Angel, has a favorite toy that she has slept with since she arrived at our home as an eight week old playful puppy. In two years, that toy is completely worn and I have been unable to find another to replace it. So, I am hoping that she will love this replacement toy as much as the original.

Approximate Size: 10" long

Materials
fat quarter brown flannel
fat quarter pink fleece or terrycloth
polyester fiberfil

Patterns
Ice Cream Cone (page 112)
Ice Cream Half-Circle (page 113)

Cutting
1 Ice Cream cone, brown flannel
1 Ice Cream Circle, pink fleece or terrycloth

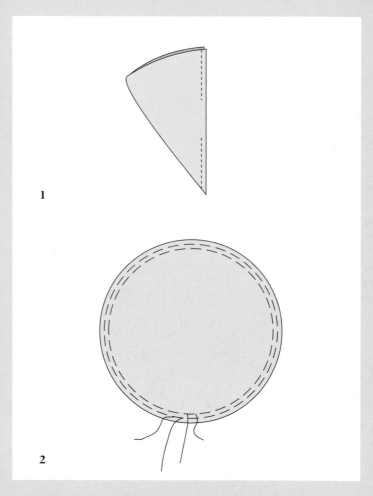

Instructions

1. Fold Ice Cream Cone in half with right sides together; sew along straight edge leaving a 3" opening. **(Diagram 1)**

2. Using a long basting stitch, sew 1/4" and 1/2" from raw edge of Ice Cream Circle. **(Diagram 2)**

3. Gather Ice Cream Circle by pulling thread ends and place gathered Circle inside Ice Cream Cone with right sides together. Pin in place matching raw edges. Sew together using a 1/2" seam allowance.

4. Turn Ice Cream Cone right side out through opening. Stuff Cone with polyester fiberfil.

5. Handstitch opening closed.

Your Ice Cream toy is ready to be enjoyed by your favorite pooch.

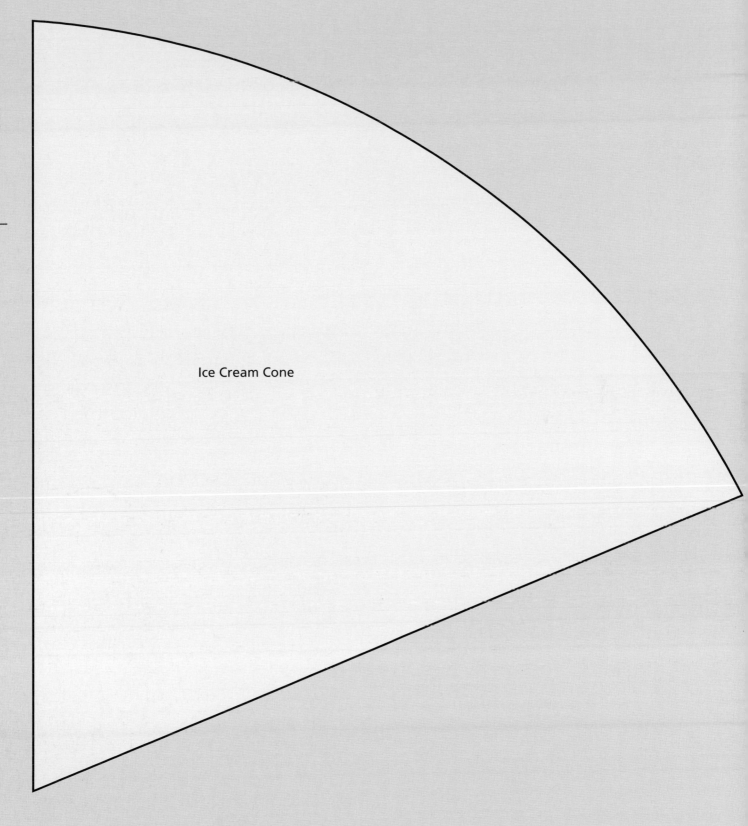

Ice Cream Cone

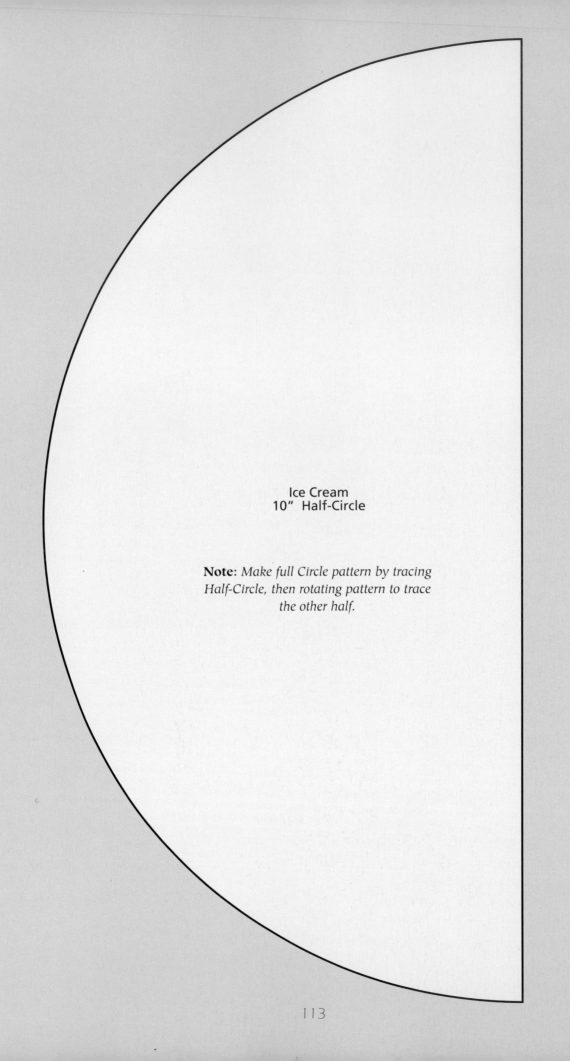

Ice Cream
10" Half-Circle

Note: *Make full Circle pattern by tracing Half-Circle, then rotating pattern to trace the other half.*

Magic Jacket

With a bit of sewing magic, you can turn a plain sweatshirt into a lovely jacket.

time to make:
about 7 hours

Materials

1 black sweatshirt (Use a sweatshirt with set-in, not raglan, sleeves.)

*fabric strips in various widths, shades of blue, purple, pink, yellow, green, and aqua

2/3 yard coordinating fabric (bias strips) or purchased bias tape

4 buttons, 1" diameter

1 yard flat cording

acrylic ruler

fabric marking pen or pencil (use white for dark sweatshirt)

*The photographed jacket uses approximately 60 different fabric prints.

Cutting

Jacket Front and Sleeves

Cut 12" long strips in the assorted widths:

3/4" x 12"

1" x 12"

1¼" x 12"
1½" x 12"
1¾" x 12"
2" x 12"
02¼" x 12"
Trim
2½"-wide bias strips

Instructions

Sewing Strip Sets

1. Divide fabric strips in groups of color—blue, purple, pink, yellow, green and aqua.

2. Sew blue strips together randomly until you have a strip set with a minimum width of 18". (**Diagram 1**) Press seams to one side.

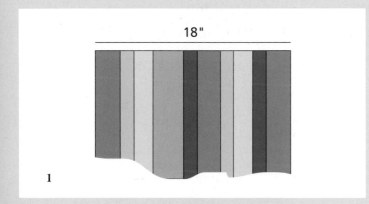

18"

1

3. Repeat step 2 for remaining five color groups.

4. Cut two strips each, 1¼", 1¾" and 2¼" wide from all strip sets. (**Diagram 2**)

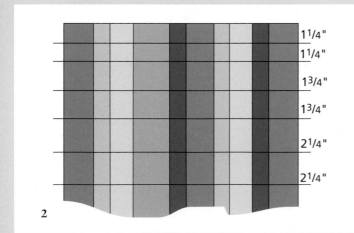

1¼"
1¼"
1¾"
1¾"
2¼"
2¼"

2

Preparing the Sweatshirt

1. Cut off neck, sleeve and lower edge band near seams. (**Diagram 3**)

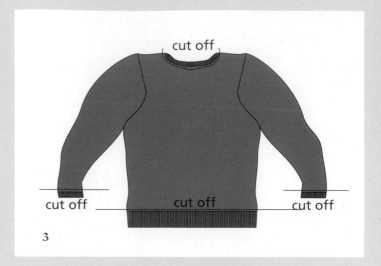

cut off

cut off   cut off   cut off

3

2. Lay sweatshirt on a flat surface with front facing up. Mark center from neck to lower edge using ruler and marking pencil. (**Diagram 4**)

4

3. Cut along marked line on sweatshirt front only.

4. Cut seams from sides and sleeves cutting as close as possible to each side of seam (**Diagram 5**)

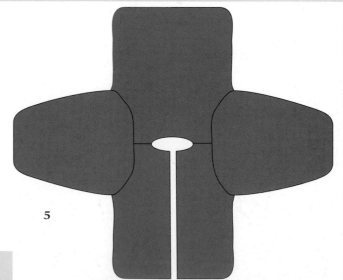

5

Finishing Jacket

1. Divide strips so you have two piles with the same strips in each. Place first strip right side up on sweatshirt front going diagonally from top corner to top edge of side. **(Diagram 6)** Pin strip in place.
Hint: *Use a glue stick to adhere strip to sweatshirt instead of using pins.*

2. Place next strip right side together with first strip and lower raw edges even. **(Diagram 7)**

3. Using your presser foot as a guide, sew strips together using a 1/4" seam allowance. **(Diagram 8)**

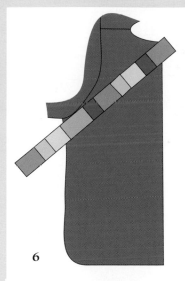

6

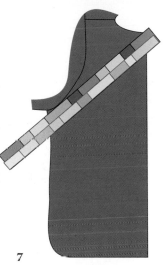

7

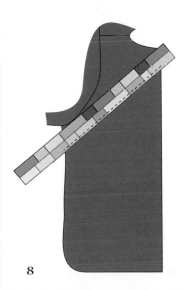

8

4. Fold just sewn strip over and press. **(Diagram 9)**

5. Continue sewing strips in this manner until completely covered. **(Diagram 10)**

6. Repeat on other front side, sewing strips in the same color order as first side.

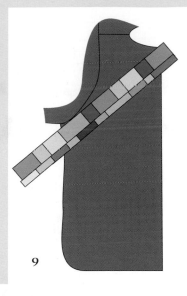

9

10

7. Trim strips even with shirt edges. **(Diagram 11)**

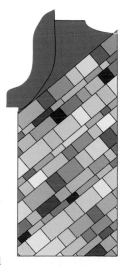

11

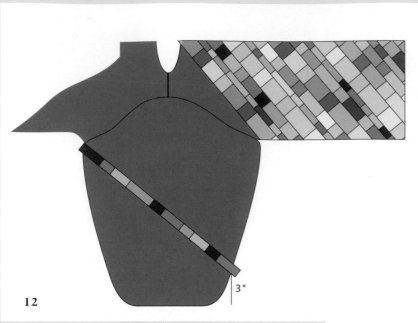

12

3"

8. For sleeves, measure 3" up from lower right edge of right sleeve. Place a 1¹/₄"-wide pieced strip starting at the 3" mark and going diagonally upward toward the top edge of the opposite side of the sleeve. (**Diagram 12**) Pin in place.

9. Place another 1¹/₄" strip right side down with pinned strip and sew along lower edge with a ¹/₄" seam allowance. (**Diagram 13**)

10. Fold top strip open. (**Diagram 14**)

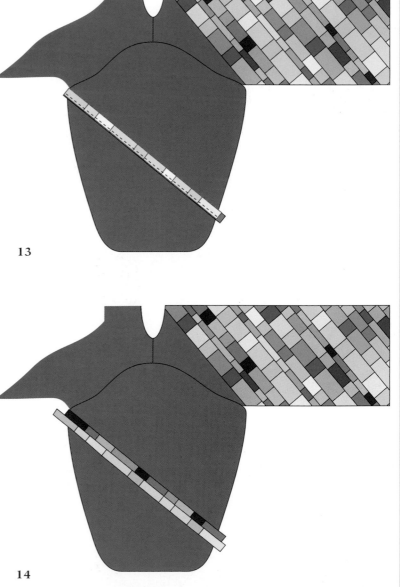

13

14

11. Fold the lengthwise raw edge of each strip under 1/4". Machine stitch near fold along lengths of strip. **(Diagram 15)** Trim edges of strips even with sleeve edge.

12. Repeat steps 8 to 11 on other sleeve making first mark 3" from lower left edge. **(Diagram 16)**

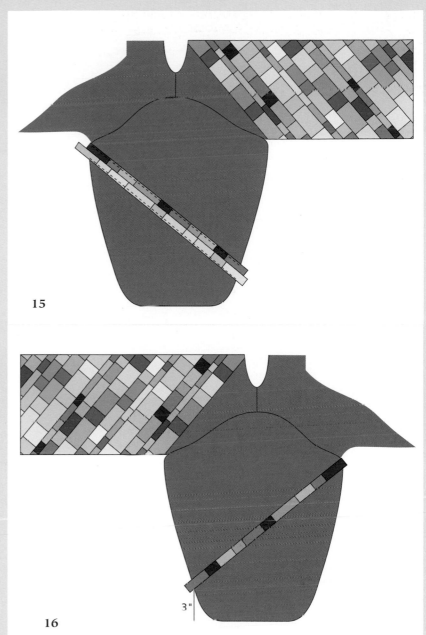

15

16

3"

13. For sleeve hem, place a 2¼" pieced strip with right side of strip together with wrong side of lower edge of sleeve. Sew with a ¼" seam allowance. (**Diagram 17**)

14. Fold remaining long edge of pieced strip under ¼" and press. (**Diagram 18**)

15. Fold pieced strip toward right side of sleeve and press. Sew folded edge of strip to sleeve. Trim strips even with sleeve edges. (**Diagram 19**)

16. Repeat steps 13 to 15 on other sleeve.

17. Sew jacket together at starting at sides and going up toward end of sleeves using a ½" seam allowance. Finish seam edges with a small zigzag stitch.

18. For Jacket edging, Refer to Making Bias Strips, page 142. Cut a 24" square then cut 2½"-wide strips to total about 120".

19. Fold bias strip in half lengthwise with wrong sides together.

20. Refer to Attaching the Continuous Binding, page 141, to attach bias strip to edge of jacket. Starting at wrong side of lower back edge, sew bias strip to back, continuing toward front, up front edge, around neck, down other side and finishing at lower back edge.

21. Fold bias strip toward front and sew in place along fold using matching thread.

22. Sew buttons to front of jacket starting at top and then about 4" to 5" between remaining buttons.

23. Cut 3" pieces of flat cording. Fold cording in half and sew to back of opposite jacket font matching spacing of buttons.

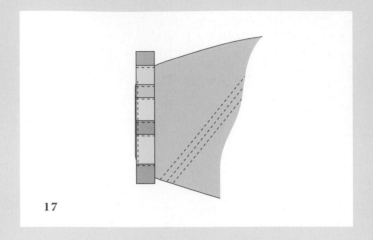

17

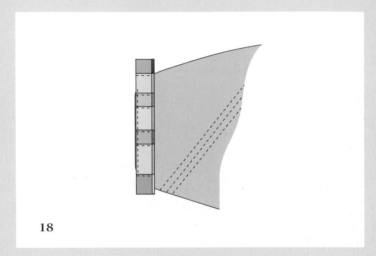

18

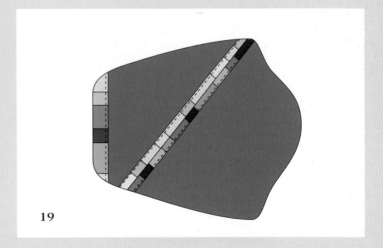

19

Book Covers

The perfect gift for a person who loves to read and treasures her books.

time to make: about 1 hour

Materials

Note: *The instructions are for standard-size paperbacks. If making a cover for a larger paperback, you will need up to 1/2 yard each of print, lining and Fast-2-Fuse™.*

fat quarter print fabric
fat quarter lining fabric
1/3 yard Fast-2-Fuse™ heavyweight fusible interfacing
2/3 yard 1/4"-wide satin or grosgrain ribbon

Instructions

1. Measure book from top to bottom and from edge of front around to edge of back to get a length and width measurement. (**Diagram 1**)

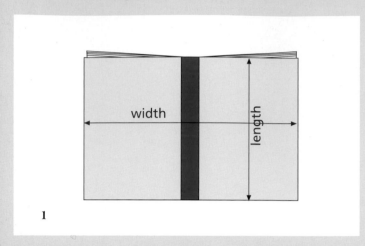

1

2. Add ¹/₂" to the lengthwise measurement and 6" to the width and cut print, lining and Fast-2-Fuse™. (**Diagram 2**)

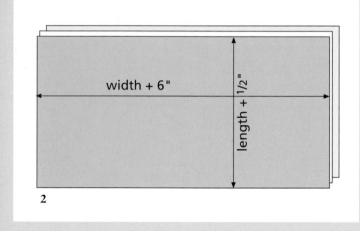

2

3. Refer to manufacturer's directions and fuse the lining and print to opposite sides of the Fast-2-Fuse™.

4. Set your sewing machine to a tight zigzag (satin) and stitch along both short sides. Fold each side edge 3" toward lining. (**Diagram 3**)

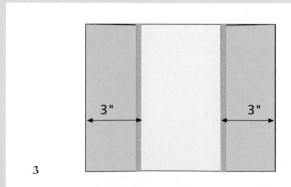

3

5. Sew along top and bottom edges with a tight zigzag stitch. (**Diagram 4**)

4

6. Cut a piece of ribbon about 1" longer than the length of the book and sew at top center.

7. Cut remaining ribbon in half and sew each piece to center of side edges. (**Diagram 5**)

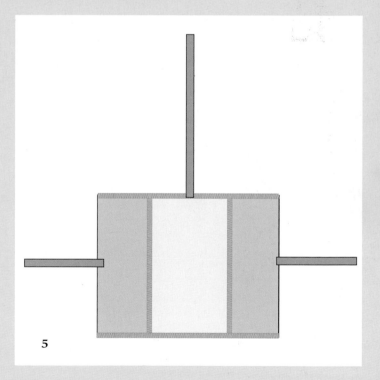

5

Quilt of Cars

If you find car fabric, you should certainly make this quilt for a car fanatic or make the quilt with other favorite fabrics.

time to make: about 15 hours

Approximate Size: 76" x 93"

Materials

2¹/2 yards car print 1
3 yards car print 2 (includes second border)
1¹/2 yards black/white check
1¹/4 yards green print (includes first border)
6 yards backing fabric
5/8 yard binding
twin-size fusible batting

Cutting

Blocks

    12 strips, 3¹/2"-wide, car print 2 (Block A)
    12 strips, 3¹/2"-wide, black/white check (Block A)
    3 strips, 3¹/2"-wide, green print (Block A)
    31 squares, 9¹/2" x 9¹/2", car print 1 (Block B)

*Optional cutting: *If you would like to sew with squares rather than strips, then cut the following for Block A:*

    124 squares, 3¹/2" x 3¹/2", car print 2
    124 squares, 3¹/2" x 3¹/2", black/white check
    32 squares, 3¹/2" x 3¹/2", green print

Finishing

    8 strips, 2"-wide, green print (first border)
    8 strips, 5¹/2"-wide, car print 2 (second border)
    8 strips, 2¹/2"-wide, black/white check (binding)

Instructions

1. Sew 3½"-wide car print 2 strip to opposite sides of a 3½"-wide black/white check strips. Press seams to one side. (**Diagram 1**) Repeat for 5 more strip sets

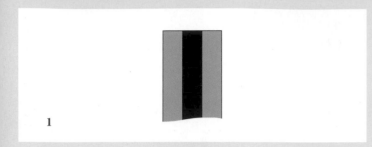

1

2. Sew 3½"-wide black/white check strip to opposite sides of a 3½"-wide green print strip. Press seams to opposite side of strips from step 1. (**Diagram 2**)

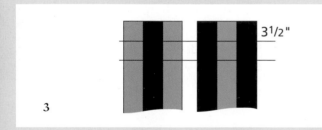

2

3. Cut strip sets at 3½" intervals. (**Diagram 3**)

3½"

3

4. Sew strips together to form a Nine Patch. (**Diagram 4**) Make 32 Nine Patch Block A.

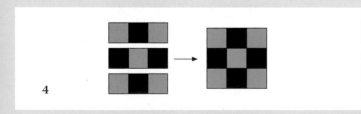

4

5. Place Block A and Block B alternating in nine rows of seven blocks. Sew blocks together in rows; press seams toward plain Block B. (**Diagram 5**) Sew rows together.

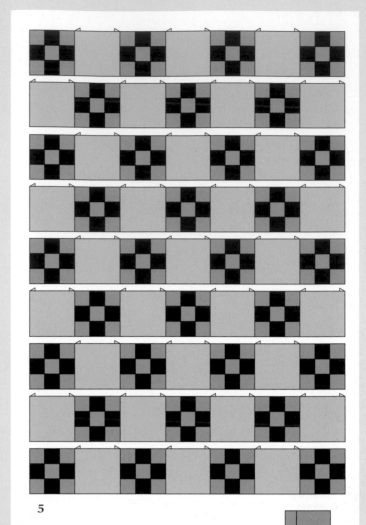

5

6. Measure quilt top lengthwise. Sew two 2"-wide green print strips together to form one long strip; repeat for a second strip. Cut both strips to equal the lengthwise measurement. Repeat for the 5½"-wide car print 2 strips.

7. Sew a 2"-wide green print strip to a 5½"-wide car print 2 strip along length; repeat with remaining two strips. (**Diagram 6**)

6

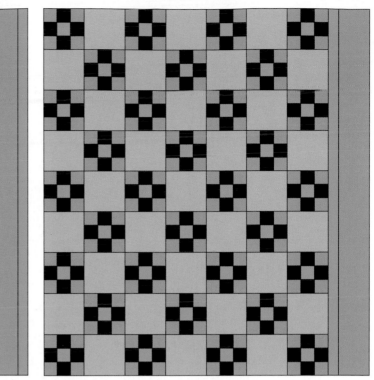

8. Sew strips to sides of quilt top with green strip next to quilt top. (**Diagram 7**) Press seams toward borders.

9. Measure quilt top crosswise. Sew two 2"-wide green print strips together to form one long strip; repeat for a second strip. Cut both strips to equal the crosswise measurement. Repeat for the 5¹/2"-wide car print 2 strips.

10. Sew a 2"-wide green print strip to a 5¹/2"-wide car print 2 strip along length; repeat with remaining two strips.

11. Sew strips to top and bottom of quilt top with green strip next to quilt top. (**Diagram 8**) Press seams toward borders.

12. Cut backing fabric in half across width. Remove selvages from both pieces. Sew pieces together along length. Press seam open.

13. Place backing wrong side up on a flat surface. Spread batting on top. Center quilt top over batting and smooth out. Follow manufacturer's directions to fuse batting to quilt top and backing.

14. Quilt as desired. Attach binding referring to Attaching Continuous Binding, page 141.

7

8

124

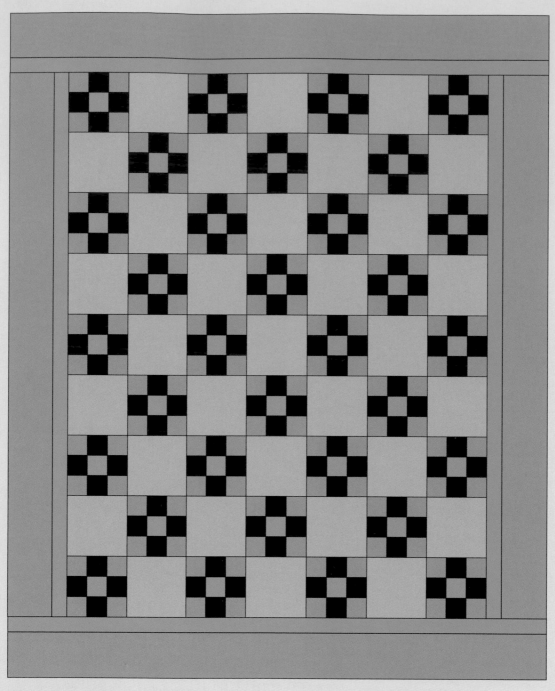

Quilt of Cars Layout

Yoyo Vest

Use pre-made yoyos to create a one-of-a-kind vest for a favorite person.

time to make: about 6 hours

Approximate Size: Small

Materials
208 pre-made yoyos, 2" diameter
invisible or a neutral thread

Instructions

1. Place yoyos according to the charts on pages 128 and 129. **Note:** *Yoyos are placed in a random color arrangement.*

2. Place two yoyos with gathered sides together; sew for about 1" using a small machine zigzag stitch. **(Diagram 1)**

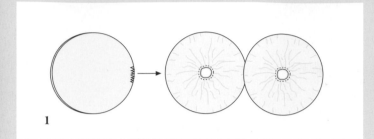

3. Continuing sewing yoyos in sections by rows, then sew rows together. **(Diagram 2)**

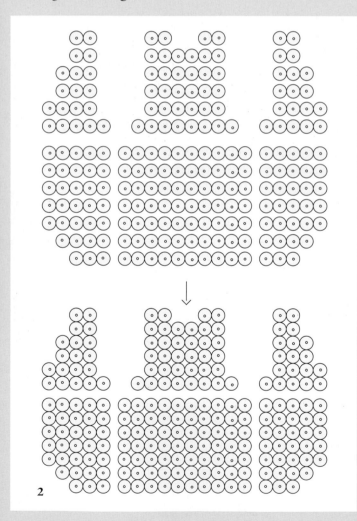

4. Sew sections together. **(Diagram 3)**

5. Sew yoyos together at shoulders. **(Diagram 4)**

6. At corners, fold yoyos in half diagonally with flat sides together. **(Diagram 5)** Tack down with a couple hand stitches.

Optional Sizes:
Follow the charts on pages 128 and 129 for medium and large sizes.

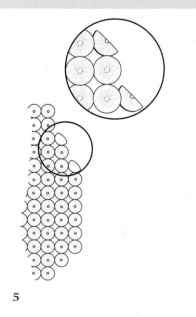

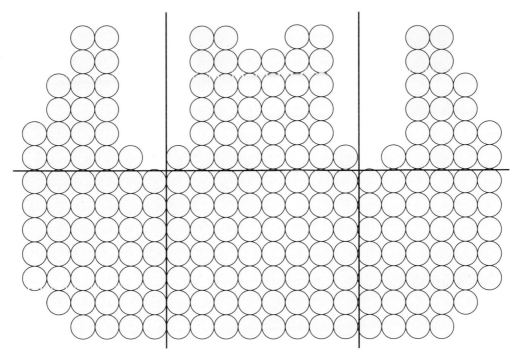

Small
208 - 2" yoyos

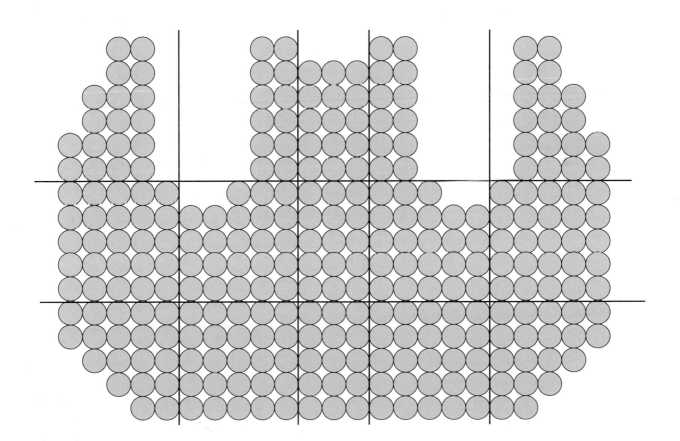

Medium
289 - 2" yoyos

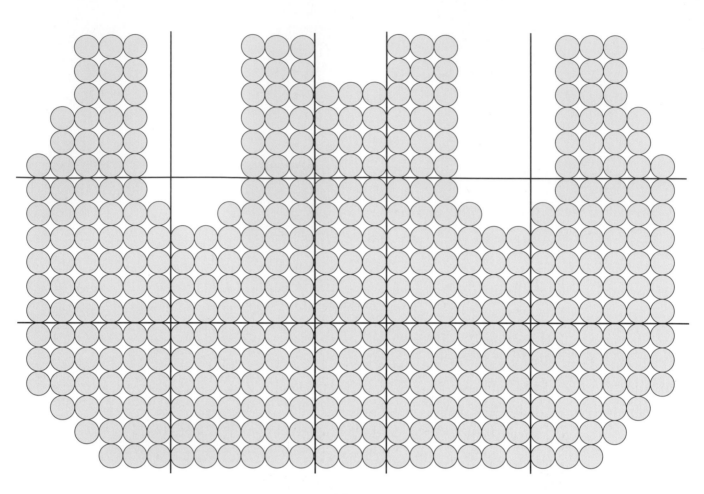

Large
392 - 2" yoyos

Optional: Making Yoyos

If you are unable to find purchased yoyos, you can make your own. Your vest will take much longer to make.

1. Fold edge of a 4 1/2" circle (for 2" finished yoyo) toward wrong side about 1/8". (**Diagram 1**)

2. Thread sewing needle and knot one end using a running stitch; sew along folded edge of circle. (**Diagram 2**)

3. Pull thread to draw up circle and knot end of thread. (**Diagram 3**)

4. Flatten circle with small hole in center. (**Diagram 4**)

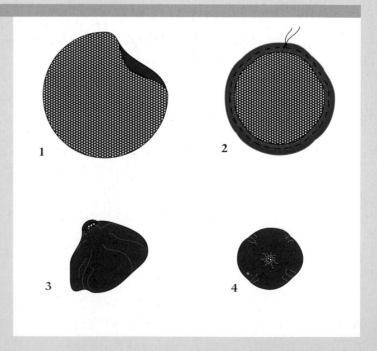

General Directions

Fabrics

Cotton

Most of the projects in this book were made using 100% cotton. There are many properties in cotton that make it especially well-suited for making a variety of projects. Cotton fabric comes in a vast assortment of prints and colors to fit anyone's taste in home decor and personal items. Cotton is easy to work with since it can be ironed flat with a steam iron; even a puckered area created by mistake, can be fixed. The sewing machine needle moves through cotton with a great deal of ease when compared to some synthetic fabrics.

For years, sewers were advised to prewash all of their fabric to test for colorfastness and shrinkage. Now, most don't bother to prewash all of their fabric but they do pretest it. Cut a strip about 2" wide from each piece of fabric that you will use in your project. Measure both the length and the width of the strip. Then immerse it in a bowl of very hot water, using a separate bowl for each piece of fabric. Be especially concerned about reds and dark blues because they have a tendency to bleed if the initial dyeing was not done properly. If it's one of your favorite fabrics that's bleeding, you might be able to salvage the fabric. Try washing the fabric in very hot water until you've washed out all of the excess dye. Unfortunately, fabrics that continue to bleed after they have been washed repeatedly will bleed forever. So you may want to eliminate them right at the start.

Now, take each one of the strips and iron it dry with a hot iron. Be especially careful not to stretch the strip. When the strips are completely dry, measure and compare them to your original strip. If all of your fabric is shrinking the same amount, you don't have to worry about uneven shrinkage in your project.

Before beginning to work, make sure that your fabric is absolutely square. If it is not, you will have difficulty cutting square pieces. Fabric is woven with crosswise and lengthwise threads. Lengthwise threads should be parallel to the selvage (that's the finished edge along the sides; sometimes the fabric company prints its name along the selvage), and crosswise threads should be perpendicular to the selvage. If fabric is off grain, you can usually straighten it by pulling gently on the true bias in the opposite direction to the off-grain edge. Continue doing this until the crosswise threads are at a right angle to the lengthwise threads.

When sewing with cotton, use a size 80 or 90 sewing machine needle and a good quality cotton or cotton wrapped polyester thread.

Working with Velvet

While velvet brings elegance to projects, it can also present some challenges. You will notice that velvet has a distinct nap so when you look at it in different directions, it can look lighter or darker. If you are working on a project where you want the velvet pieces to look the same, you must be careful to cut the individual pieces in the same direction. For the most accurate cutting, it is best to cut velvet a single thickness at a time.

Once your pieces are cut, place a size 70 needle in your machine and set your stitch length to a slightly longer stitch such as 10 stitches per inch. If your sewing machine has a walking foot, use it. If not, it is a good idea to purchase one. It will allow the fabric to feed evenly through the sewing machine. Also, hold the fabric taut while sewing and sew slowly. If the fabric starts to pucker, loosen the upper tension. Another tip to ease puckering is to stop sewing and lift the presser foot periodically. This will allow the fabric to relax before continuing on.

After sewing seams, you will want to press them with your iron. When using velvet, you cannot press the seams directly. Place velvet with right side down on a thick towel. Set your iron to a high steam setting and lightly steam the seams open. Hold the iron above the seam, barely touching the fabric. If you actually touch the velvet with the iron, you will flatten the nap of the fabric and it can never be restored to its original look. Never place an iron directly on the right side of velvet.

Fleece

Fleece has become a very popular fabric to use for a variety of items, especially for baby. Not only is the fabric soft to the touch, you can complete wonderful projects in a relatively short period of time. When buying fleece, be sure it has a non-pill finish. If you don't, your project will end up with little "balls" or "pills" on the surface that will destroy its look. When sewing fleece, you will be working with bulky seams. Use a size 70 or 80 needle in your sewing machine and good quality polyester thread. A walking foot will help feed the thick layers of fleece evenly through the sewing machine.

Flannel

Cotton flannel is a wonderfully soft fabric that is ideal for baby items and snuggly blankets or quilts. Flannel shrinks quite a bit—some more than others. So if you are using it with other fabrics, you will definitely need to prewash it. When working with flannel, use a 1/2" seam allowance since it tends to fray. You will have to clean your sewing machine often to avoid lint build up. Flannel tends to stretch, so you must adequately pin the pieces that will be sewn together so that they won't shift while sewing. Using a walking foot will also keep the fabric from shifting while sewing.

Interfacing

There are many types of interfacing on the market—lightweight, heavyweight, fusible, non-fusible, stretchy, non-stretchy.

Heavyweight interfacing is used for projects that require firm support. The two types of interfacing used in some of the 24 hour projects were Fast-2-Fuse™ and Timtex™. They have comparable thickness with the main difference being that the Fast-2-Fuse™ is fusible on both sides and the Timtex™ is not. Follow the manufacturer's directions to fuse the Fast-2-Fuse™ to fabric.

Timtex™ can be used as a fusible by using a light-weight paper-backed fusible web. Follow the manufacturer's directions and fuse the paper-backed fusible web to the wrong side of the fabric, then onto the Timtex™. Work with one side of the Timtex™ at a time.

Lightweight fusible interfacing is used in projects that require some firmness, but not the stiffness of the heavyweight interfacing. Again, follow the manufacturer's directions when using.

Paper-backed Fusible Web

There are many types of paper-backed fusible on the market. Use the lightweight types for the sewing projects in this book as they will not gum up the sewing machine needle. Follow manufacturer's directions for any product you choose as the instructions vary from type to type.

Rotary Cutting

Rotary Cutting is an easy and accurate way to cut fabric. For rotary cutting, you will need three important tools: a rotary cutter, a mat and an acrylic ruler. There are currently on the market many different brands and types. Choose the kinds that you feel will work for you. Ask your sewing friends what their preferences are, then make your decision.

There are several different rotary cutters now available with special features that you might prefer such as the type of handle, whether the cutter can be used for both right- and left-handed sewers, safety features, size, and finally, the cost.

Don't attempt to use the rotary cutter without an accompanying protective mat. The mat will not only protect your table from becoming scratched, but it will protect your cutter as well. The mat is self-healing and will not dull the cutting blades. Mats are available in many sizes, but if this is your first attempt at rotary cutting, an 18" x 24" mat is probably your best choice. When you are not using your mat, be sure to store it on a flat surface. Otherwise your mat will bend. If you want to keep your mat from warping, make certain that it is not sitting in direct sunlight; the heat can cause the mat to warp. You will not be able to cut accurately when you use a bent or warped mat.

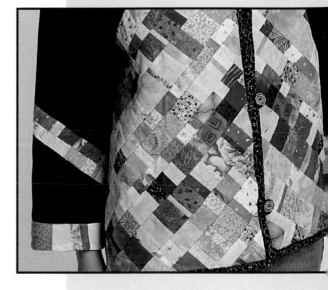

Another must for cutting accurate strips is a strong straight edge. Acrylic rulers are the perfect choice for this. There are many different brands of acrylic rulers on the market, and they come in several widths and lengths. Either a 6" x 24" or a 6" x 12" ruler will be the most useful. The longer ruler will allow you to fold your fabric only once while the smaller size will require folding the fabric twice. Make sure that your ruler has 1/8" increment markings in both directions plus a 45-degree marking.

Cutting Strips With a Rotary Cutter

Before beginning to work, iron your fabric to remove the wrinkles. Fold the fabric in half, lengthwise, bringing the selvage edges together. Fold in half again. Make sure that there are no wrinkles in the fabric.

Now place the folded fabric on the cutting mat. Place the fabric length on the right side if you are right-handed or on the left side if you are left-handed. The fold of the fabric should line up along one of the grid lines printed on the mat. (**Diagram 1**)

Straighten one of the cut edges first. Lay the acrylic ruler on the mat near the cut edge; the ruler markings should be even with the grid on the mat. Hold the ruler firmly with your left hand (or, with your right hand if you are left-handed). To provide extra stability, keep your small finger off the mat. Now hold the rotary cutter with blade against the ruler and cut away from you in one quick motion. (**Diagram 2**)

Carefully turn the fabric (or mat with the fabric) so the straightened edge is on the opposite side. Place the ruler on the required width line along the cut edge of the fabric and cut the strip, making sure that you always cut away from you—never toward you. Cut the number of strips called for in the directions. (**Diagram 3**)

After you have cut a few strips, you will want to check to make certain that your fabric continues to be perfectly square. To do this, just line up the crosswise markings along the folded edge of fabric and the lengthwise edge of the ruler next to the end of fabric you are cutting. Cut off uneven edge. If you fail to do this, your strips may be bowed with a "v" in the center, causing your piecing to become inaccurate as you continue working.

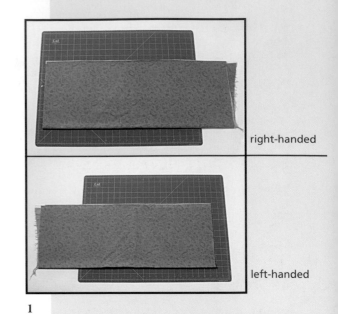

right-handed

left-handed

1

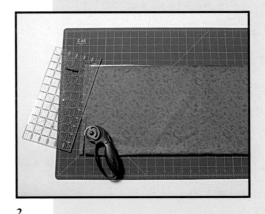

2

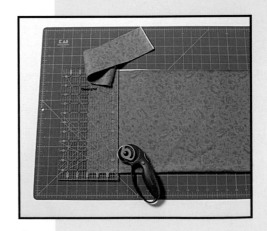

3

Cutting Squares and Rectangles

Now that you have cut your strips, you can begin to cut squares or rectangles. Place a stack of strips on the cutting mat. You will be more successful in cutting—at least in the beginning—if you work with no more than four strips at a time. Make certain that the strips are lined up very evenly. Following the instructions given for the project, cut the required number of squares or rectangles. **(Diagram 4)**

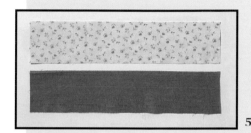

4

Piecing Techniques

Strip Piecing

Strip piecing is a much faster and easier method of working rather than creating blocks piece by piece. With this method, two or more strips are sewn together and then cut at certain intervals. For instance, if a block is made up of several 3" finished squares, cut 3 1/2"-wide strips along the crosswise grain. **(Diagram 5)**

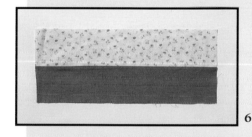

5

With right sides together, sew two strips along the length. The seam should be pressed toward the dark side of the fabric. **(Diagram 6)**

Cut across strips at 3 1/2" intervals. **(Diagram 7)** This will create 3" finished squares.

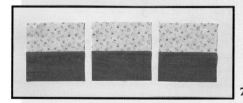

6

Chain Piecing

Chain piecing is a way to sew similar units quickly and accurately. If you are making a project such as a quilt that has several squares that need to be sewn together, you can sew pairs of squares continuously through the sewing machine without lifting your presser foot.

7

Place two squares right sides together and sew along one edge using a 1/4" seam allowance; do not backstitch. **(Diagram 8)** Do not remove from sewing machine and do not lift presser foot.

8

Place another pair of squares right sides together; butt up against squares just sewn and continue sewing. (**Diagram 9**) Continue feeding pairs of squares under the presser until all the squares sewn together.

Take the entire sewn "chain" to the ironing board and press seams in one direction, usually toward the darker fabric.

Clip threads between sewn pairs.

Making a Quilt

Sewing Blocks Together

Once you have sewn all the blocks required for your quilt according to the individual project instructions, press them carefully. Measure the blocks to make sure they are all the same size. Even with the most careful sewing, blocks can vary slightly in size. It is easier to trim larger blocks than it is to make a block larger. Find the smallest size and trim all blocks to that size. If the blocks vary in size by more than 1/4", you may want to unsew a few seams and sew those pieces back together again.

Adding Simple Borders

Measure the quilt top lengthwise and cut two border strips to that length by the width measurement given in the project instructions. (**Diagram 10**)

Strips may have to be pieced to achieve the correct length. To make the joining seam less noticeable, sew the strips together diagonally. Place two strips right sides together at right angles. Sew a diagonal seam. (**Diagram 11**).

Trim excess fabric 1/4" from stitching. (**Diagram 12**)

Press seam open. (**Diagram 13**)

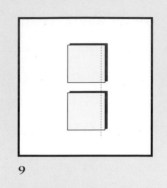

9

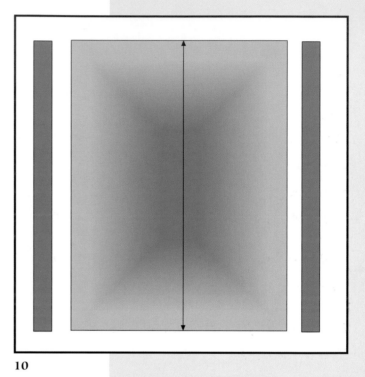

10

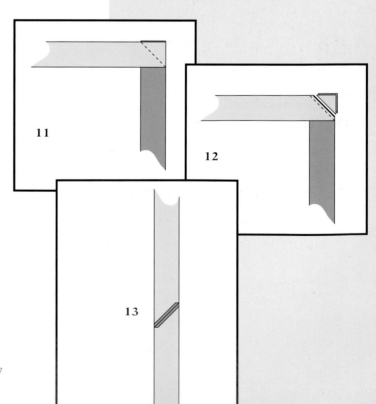

11

12

13

Sew strips to the sides of the quilt and press seams toward the border strip. Now measure the quilt top crosswise, being sure to include the borders you have just added. Cut two border strips, following the width measurement given in the instructions. (**Diagram 14**)

Add these borders to the top and bottom of the quilt and press seams toward border strip. Repeat this process for any additional borders. Use the 1/4" seam allowance at all times and press all of the seams to the darker side. Press the quilt top carefully.

Attaching the Batting and Backing

There are a number of different types of batting on the market today including the new fusible battings that eliminate the need for basting. Your choice of batting will depend upon how you are planning to use your quilt. If the quilt is to serve as a wall hanging, you will probably want to use a thin cotton batting. A quilt made with a thin cotton or cotton/polyester blend works best for machine quilting. Very thick polyester batting should be used only for tied quilts.

The best fabric for quilt backing is 100% cotton fabric. If your quilt is larger than the available fabric you will have to piece your backing fabric. When joining the fabric, try not to have a seam going down the center. Instead cut off the selvages and make a center strip that is about 36" wide and have narrower strips at the sides. Seam the pieces together and carefully iron the seams open. (This is one of the few times in making a quilt that a seam should be pressed open.) Several fabric manufacturers are now selling fabric in 90" or 108"-widths for use as backing fabric.

It is a good idea to remove the batting from its wrapping 24 hours before you plan to use it and open it out to full size. You will find that the batting will now lie flat when you are ready to use it.

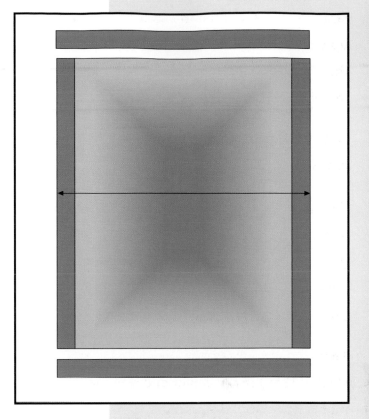

14

The batting and the backing should be cut about one to two inches larger on all sides than the quilt top. Place the backing wrong side up on a flat surface. Smooth out the batting on top of this, matching the outer edges. Center the quilt top, right side up, on top of the batting.

Now the quilt layers must be held together before quilting, and there are several methods for doing this:

Safety-pin Basting: Starting from the center and working toward the edges, pin through all layers at one time with large safety pins. The pins should be placed no more than 4" apart. As you work, think of your quilting plan to make sure that the pins will avoid prospective quilting lines.

Thread Basting: Baste the three layers together with long stitches. Start in the center and sew toward the edges in a number of diagonal lines.

Quilt-gun Basting: This handy trigger tool pushes nylon tags through all layers of the quilt. Start in the center and work toward the outside edges. The tags should be placed about 4" apart. You can sew right over the tags, which can then be easily removed by cutting them off with scissors.

Spray or Heat-Set Basting: Several manufacturers have spray adhesives available especially for quilters. Apply these products by following the manufacturers' directions. You might want to test these products before you use them to make sure that they meet your requirements.

Fusible Iron-on Batting: These battings are a wonderful new way to hold quilt layers together without using any of the other time-consuming methods of basting. Again, you will want to test these battings to be certain that you are happy with the results. Follow the manufacturers' directions.

Quilting

If you like the process of hand quilting, you can—of course—finish your projects by hand quilting. However, if you want to finish these quilts quickly, in the time we are suggesting, you will want to use a sewing machine for quilting.

If you have never used a sewing machine for quilting, you may want to find a book and read about the technique. You do not need a special machine for quilting. Just make sure that your machine has been oiled and is in good working condition.

If you are going to do machine quilting, you should invest in an even-feed foot. This foot is designed to feed the top and bottom layers of a quilt evenly through the machine. The foot prevents puckers from forming as you machine quilt. Use a fine transparent nylon thread in the top and regular sewing thread in the bobbin.

Quilting in the ditch is one of the easiest ways to machine quilt. This is a term used to describe stitching along the seam line between two pieces of fabric. Using your fingers, pull the blocks or pieces apart slightly and machine stitch right between the two pieces. The stitching will look better if you keep the stitching to the side of the seam that does not have the extra bulk of the seam allowance under it. The quilting will be hidden in the seam.

Free-form machine quilting can be used to quilt around a design or to quilt a motif. The quilting is done with a darning foot and the feed dogs down on the sewing machine. It takes practice to master Free-form quilting because you are controlling the movement of the quilt under the needle rather than the sewing machine moving the quilt. You can quilt in any direction—up and down, side-to-side and even in circles—without pivoting the quilt around the needle. Practice this quilting method before trying it on your quilt.

Attaching the Continuous Binding

Once the project has been quilted, it must be bound to cover the raw edges.

Start by trimming the backing and batting even with the top. Measure the top and cut enough 2½"-wide strips to go around all four sides plus 12". Join the strips end to end with diagonal seams and trim the corners. Press the seams open. (**Diagram 15**)

Cut one end of the strip at a 45-degree angle and press under ¼". Press entire strip in half lengthwise, wrong sides together.(**Diagram 16**)

On the back, position the binding in the middle of one side, keeping the raw edges together. Sew the binding with the ¼" seam allowance, beginning about three inches below the folded end of the binding. (**Diagram 17**) At the corner, stop ¼" from the edge of the project and backstitch.

Fold binding away from the project so it is at a right angle to edge just sewn. Then, fold the binding back on itself so the fold is on the edge and the raw edges are aligned with the adjacent side. Begin sewing at the edge. (**Diagram 18**)

Continue in the same way around the remaining sides of the project. Stop about 2" away from the starting point. Trim any excess binding and tuck it inside the folded end. Finish the stitching. (**Diagram 19**)

Fold the binding to the front of the project so the seam line is covered; machine-stitch the binding in place on the front of the project. Use a straight stitch or tiny zigzag with invisible or matching thread. If you have a sewing machine that does embroidery stitches, you may want to use your favorite stitch.

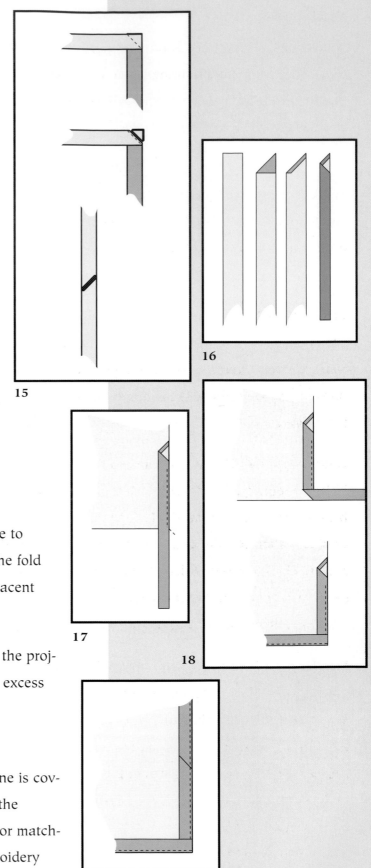

15

16

17

18

19

Making Bias Strips

Sometimes you will need to use bias strips to finish a project, for example, binding the edges of the Sweatshirt Jacket, page 114. Bias strips are used when you need to go around curved edges.

To make the strips, you need to start out with a square of fabric. For smaller projects, you will need a square that is at least 18" x 18". You will get about 90" of 2½"-wide bias strips from an 18" square. A 24" square will make about 120" of 2½"-wide bias strips.

Using a ruler and a fabric marking pencil, draw 45 degree diagonal lines across the square. (**Diagram 20**) **Note**: *It is important that the lines are at a 45 degree angle to achieve strips that are along the true bias.*

Cut along the drawn lines. (**Diagram 21**)

Place two strips right sides together at a right angle. Slide ends so that small triangles are formed that extend about ½" from each end. (**Diagram 22**) Pin in place.

Sew strips together beginning and ending where strips intersect. (**Diagram 23**) Press seam open.

Continue sewing strips together until desired length is achieved.

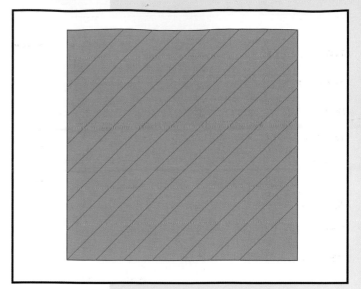

20

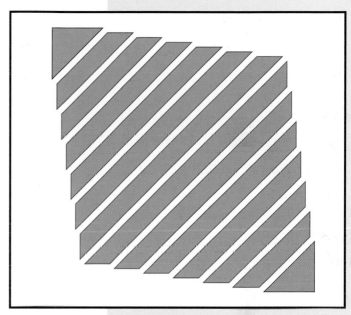

21

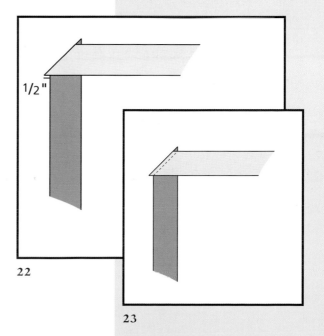

1/2"

22

23

Adding a Rod Pocket

In order to hang a quilt or another project, you will need to attach a rod pocket to the back.

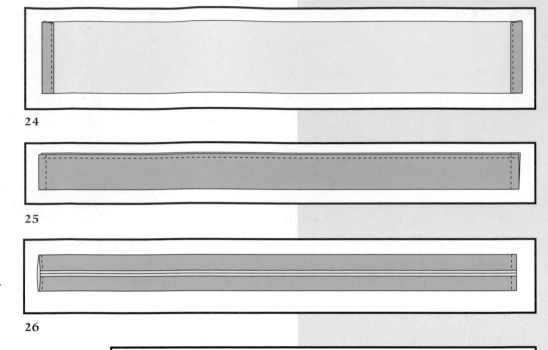

24

Cut a strip of fabric, 6" wide by the width of the project.

25

Fold short ends of strip under ¼", then fold another ¼". Sew along first fold. **(Diagram 24)**

26

Fold strip lengthwise with wrong sides together. Sew along raw edges with a ¼" seam allowance to form a long tube. **(Diagram 25)**

Press seam open and resulting tube flat. **(Diagram 26)**

Place tube on back of the project, seam side against project, about 1" from top edge and equal distant from side edges. **(Diagram 27)** Pin in place so tube is straight across project.

Hand stitch top and bottom edges of tube to back of the project being careful not to let stitches show on front of the project.

27

Index

Metric Equivalents

inches	cm	inches	cm	inches	cm
1	2.54	11	27.94	21	53.34
2	5.08	12	30.48	22	55.88
3	7.62	13	33.02	23	58.42
4	10.16	14	35.56	24	60.96
5	12.70	15	38.10	30	76.20
6	15.24	16	40.64	36	91.44
7	17.78	17	43.18	42	106.68
8	20.32	18	45.72	48	121.92
9	22.86	19	48.26	54	137.16
10	25.40	20	50.8	60	152.40